FLAT: #2, #4 and 1"
Use flat brushes for basecoating, drybrushing, washing glazes and varnishing.

LINER: #10/0
I like to use a very thin liner of medium length. This is used for outlining and fine linework like eyes, eyelashes, etc.

RAKE: 1/4"
Use this brush to paint fur, feathers and grass.

ROUND: #3, #6, #10, #12
Use the round brushes to basecoat areas that are hard to reach with a flat brush. They can also be used for highlighting and blending.

SMUDGE TINT: #4, #8
Wow, this is a fabulous brush. It is used for scumbling or rubbing highlights and shadows to create form. The brush is also called a "smooshing" brush. Mine is a Designer Brush Series BR570. An alternative would be a small, round, bristle brush, like an Eterna China bristle.

SABLE
REKAB SERIES 337 ROUND: #4
This brush is used for all the lettering throughout the book. This brush has a square, chiselled-edge tip that is needed to form precise letter shapes.

GENERAL SUPPLIES

Art gum eraser
Hair dryer (optional, for force drying)
Jo Sonja's All Purpose Sealer
Jo Sonja's Polyurethane Water Based Satin Varnish
Jo Sonja's Retarder Medium
Old toothbrush (optional, for flyspecking)
Paper towels
Sandpaper, fine-grade
Soft, lint-free cloths
Stylus
Tack cloth
Tile (optional)
Tracing paper
Transfer paper, white and grey
Water container
Wet palette

Please check individual projects for additional supplies.

Wood Source
Viking Woodcrafts, Inc.
1317 8th St. S.E.
Waseca, MN 56093   PH: (800) 328-0116
Web site: http://www.vikingwoodcrafts.com
Wooden Basket #25-0042, Plates #18-1705

General Instructions

WOOD PREPARATION:
PINE: I like the look of wood grain, so I choose pieces made from pine. To prepare, lightly sand the wood in the direction of the grain with fine-grade sandpaper. Remove any dust with a tack cloth. I don't use sealer, but you may if you prefer. I don't mix any mediums into the paint; instead, I thin the paint with water to allow the wood grain to show through the basecoat. Use the 1" flat brush to basecoat the piece with the desired Jo Sonja paint colour.

CRAFTWOOD: I use two methods for preparing craftwood (compressed particleboard).

Method #1: I use this method when I want the background paint to appear slightly transparent. Apply two coats of Jo Sonja's All Purpose Sealer before basecoating, allowing time for each coat to dry and sanding the surface only if necessary.

Method #2: I use the second method when I want solid, opaque colour. Before applying the basecoat colour, thin Jo Sonja's Gesso with water and basecoat the piece with two coats of gesso, using the 1" flat brush. This gives the surface some tooth for the paint to grip and helps seal any impurities into the wood. After preparing the surface with gesso, scoop the specified background colour onto a tile and thin it with water. Apply paint using the 1" flat brush, allowing each coat to dry thoroughly before applying another. I only sand the surface between coats if the paint has been applied a little too thickly, causing ridges to form. The moral is, if you are careful, you won't need to sand.

TRANSFERRING THE PATTERN: Trace the pattern onto a piece of tracing paper. Position the tracing on the surface of the project and secure with tape. Place a piece of transfer paper under the tracing, waxy side down, and lightly trace over the main pattern lines using a stylus. Use the white transfer paper for dark surfaces and the grey for lighter surfaces. Transfer the details as needed.

FINISHING: Allow time for the paint to cure. Erase all transfer lines with an art gum eraser. Apply several coats of Jo Sonja's Polyurethane Satin Varnish with the 1" flat brush, allowing each coat to dry between applications.

Terms and Techniques

DIRTY BRUSH: To facilitate the transition between colours, I don't wash my brush between colour changes. Instead, I wipe excess paint from the brush on a cloth before picking up a new colour. When the brush becomes too dry, tip it into water, but don't wash the previous colour out.

DRYBRUSHING: Drybrushing is a technique used to render soft detail and texture. It involves painting with the barest minimum of paint on the brush so that the colour only partially covers the colour underneath. It takes some practice; if there is not enough paint on the brush, it will not release onto the surface, but if there is too much, it will make a blotchy mess. Moisten the recommended brush with water,

(Continued on Page 5)

4

Ducklings with Vegetables
Pages 6-8

Foreword

I am undoubtedly a lover of all things "country."

The country look is more than a way of decorating my home. It has translated itself into my life style. My husband and I recently fulfilled a lifetime dream of building a wonderful country home. We have lots of "green" space (25 acres) for our children to roam. We keep chickens or "chooks" as they are affectionately called here. We are reaping the rewards of organic gardening. We grow our own vegetables and are enjoying adding new gardens around our home, learning through trial and error.

My home is a sanctuary where my family can grow, learn, love and enjoy life's journey. Painting to me is wonderfully satisfying and fulfilling. This book is a glimpse of my "country world."

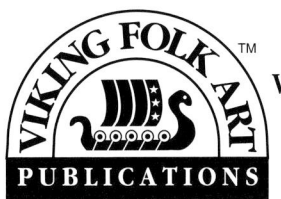

Published by
Viking Folk Art Publications, Inc.
301 16th Avenue S.E.
Waseca, MN, 56093
(507) 835-8009
Fax (507) 835-8541
E-Mail books@vikingpub.com Website: www.viking-publications.com

Dedication

I would like to dedicate this book in loving memory of my father, Terry. He was an absolute inspiration to me. He fought many tough battles throughout his life, battles that lesser mortals would not have survived. He continued to smile and make the most of what he had. He was an eternal optimist, and taught me to believe in myself and never give up. He was a true survivor and I have great admiration for him.

Society of Decorative Painters

If you enjoy decorative art and sharing painting ideas with others, please consider joining the Society of Decorative Painters. For information, write to SDP, 393 N. McLean Blvd., Wichita, Kansas 67203-5968. Web site: www.decorativepainters.org.

Copyright © 2004, Louise De Masi

All rights reserved. The designs in this book may be hand traced for personal use and hand painted for fun or profit but may not be mass produced for the wholesale market. Teachers may make one copy of a design per student, giving design credit. Other than the specified exceptions, no part of this book may be photocopied or reproduced in any mechanical form or copied in any media without the express written consent of the copyright owner.

DISCLAIMER

Publisher warrants that this book was prepared and published in good faith. However, the publisher makes no warrants either expressed or implied concerning, but not limited to, (1) the accuracy of the information contained in this book, or (2) the use, purpose, or results that may be obtained from the use of the information contained in the book. Publisher does not warrant or guarantee that the application of the information contained in this book is free from infringement of any copyright or patent held by any third party. The information or application of the information contained in this book is not intended for the use of young people or those persons who are inexperienced. Publisher's sole liability, if any, arising out of the application and use of the information contained in this book shall be limited solely to money damages not to exceed the sale price of this book. Any claim must be made in writing to the publisher within one year of the purchase of the book.

Supplies

PAINTS

Jo Sonja's® Artists' Colours, Jo Sonja's Background Colours and Matisse Artists' Colours were used for the projects in this book. Colours are listed on individual projects. The Matisse paint colour used in this book, Skintone Light, can be mixed using Jo Sonja's Skin Tone Base + Napthol Crimson (4:1).

BRUSHES

Brushes listed are suggestions only. I like to use synthetic brushes for everything except lettering. The synthetic fibres repel buildup of paint in the ferrule of the brush, and are strong and flexible. It is very important that your brushes are kept in good order. Clean them well after painting and store them so that the bristles are kept in good shape.

SYNTHETIC
ANGLED SHADER: 1/2"
Use the angled shader for floating.

DEERFOOT: #4
Use the deerfoot brush for stippling centres of sunflowers.

FAN: #3
Use for special effects. It is suitable for blending, and painting grass and foliage.

FILBERT: #6, #8
This very versatile brush gives you the benefits of a flat brush and a round brush in one. The filbert's shape gives it flexibility and spring. It is useful for basecoating, highlighting and blending.

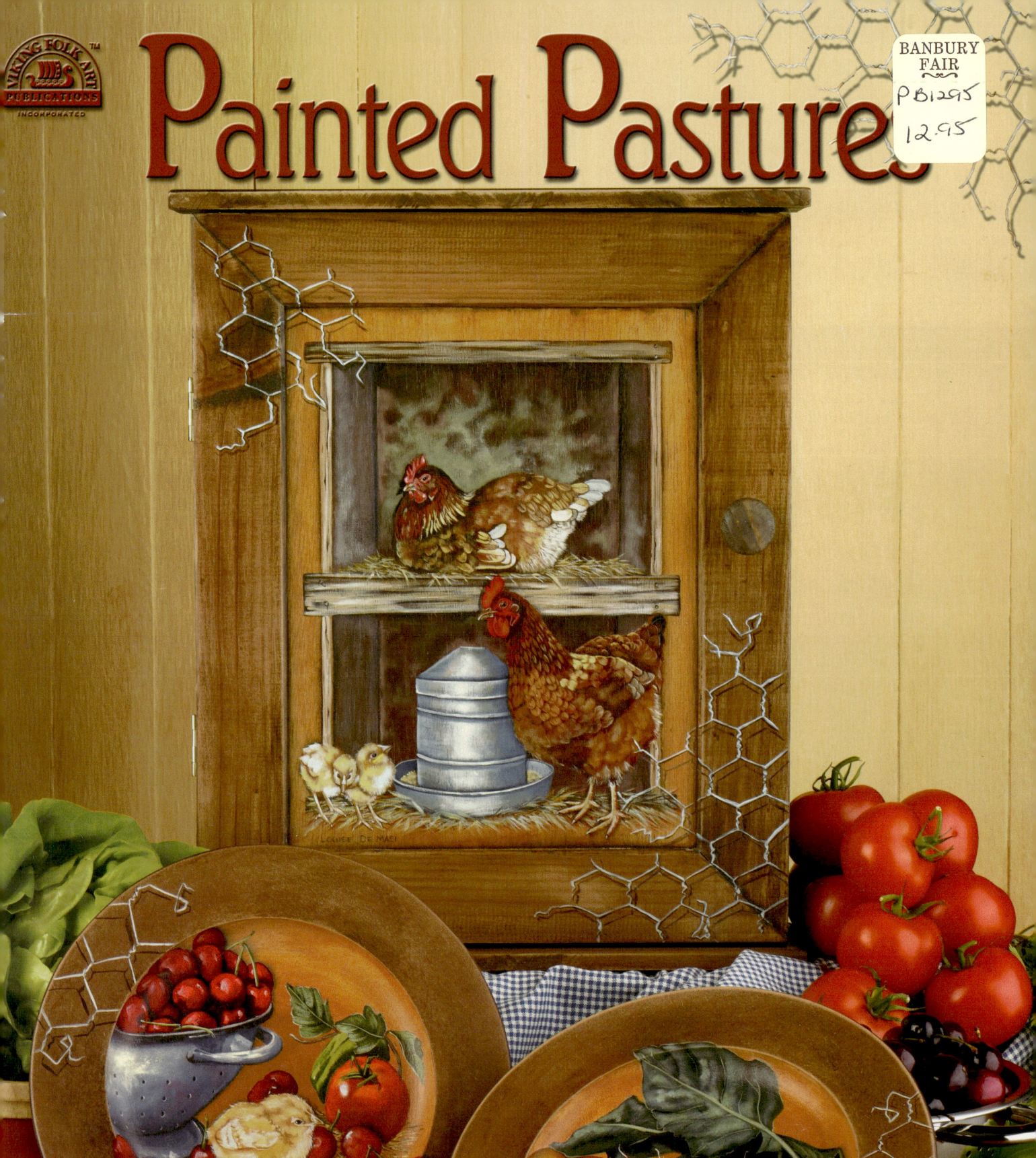

Painted Pastures

by Louise De Masi

General Instructions
(Continued from Page 3)

then blot excess water on a towel. Pick up a small amount of paint and wipe the brush again on the towel. Use very light pressure to apply the paint to the surface.

FLYSPECKING OR SPATTERING: This is an excellent, though unpredictable, method of enlivening an area of flat colour and at the same time adding that "country rustic feel" to a project. I use two methods of flyspecking.

Method #1: Thin the paint with water, then dip the bristles of an old toothbrush into the paint. "Aim" the toothbrush at the project, bristles down. Run your thumb along the bristles from front to back to flick the paint.

Method #2: This method allows a little more control. Load a large round brush with thinned paint. Hold the brush over the project, then use the handle of another large brush to tap the handle and release the paint onto the surface. Have another brush loaded with clean water ready to wipe away any specks that land where they are not intended. Be sure to wear an apron for both methods!

GLAZING: Thin the paint with water until it is the consistency of ink; use a large brush to apply this wash of colour to the surface. This transparent layer gives a lovely glow or luminosity to the design. I sometimes use this technique to brighten up the colour of leaves or petals, for instance.

LINEWORK: Thin the paint with water to inky consistency. Load the liner brush fully and then wipe excess paint on a cloth.

MIXING COLOURS: The "plus" symbol (+) between listed colours means the colours are to be mixed together. I don't mix the colours really well; I just put a puddle of each colour side by side on my palette and then use a brush to drag a small amount of each colour together (brush mixing). When I need more, I just repeat the step. The ratio listed with the colours indicates the amount of each colour to mix together.

SCUMBLING: This is a technique I use for creating texture and form. It involves scrubbing or "rubbing" full-strength paint unevenly over a layer of dry colour, allowing the first colour to partially show through. Scumbling gives amazing richness to the colours and can be applied light over dark, or dark over light. I like to use a smudge tint brush to achieve this effect. Bristle brushes can also be used as a cheaper alternative. Pick up the colour with a dry brush and use the side of the brush to rub the paint (scumble) on the surface. Imagine you are rubbing shoe polish on a pair of shoes.

SIDELOADING AND FLOATING: Dampen the angled shader (or flat) brush with water. Blot excess water on a cloth or paper towel. Dip the longest point of the angled shader (or one corner of a flat brush) into the paint, then stroke the brush in one spot on the palette, moving the bristles back and forth like a clock pendulum. The colour should be strong on the loaded side of the brush and fade to clear water on the other side. This brush is then used to float colour on the design for shadows or highlights.

SLIP-SLAP: Slip-slap is a method of applying paint in a criss-cross, carefree, loose manner. Relax and enjoy. I usually use a flat brush, and sometimes an angled shader brush.

STIPPLING: This is a method of applying the paint to create a softly textured look. Load a dry deerfoot brush with full-strength paint. Wipe excess paint from the brush on a cloth or paper towel, then apply colour by pouncing the bristles on the design surface. To add a highlight to the stippled area, allow the first colour to dry and then load the toe of the dirty brush with the highlight colour. If the paint in the brush begins to dry, wash the brush, wipe it dry, then load it again. Wipe excess paint from brush and pounce colour on the design surface to form the highlight.

TINTING: To tint a colour means to lighten it by adding white to it. I usually use Warm White and I mix the paint at a ratio of (1:1) unless otherwise specified.

USE OF MEDIUMS: I rarely use mediums other than water in my work. If I want the paint thinned, I add water until the paint is the right consistency. Jo Sonja's Retarder Medium is used in two of the projects in this book where more time is needed to blend areas where colours meet. Instructions for using retarder are listed with the project.

USING A RAKE BRUSH: I use the rake brush to paint hair, fur and feathers. The paint needs to be fairly thin, about the consistency of ink. Load the brush with paint, then wipe excess paint on a cloth. Push the bristles on the palette to separate them before applying the paint to the design surface. Holding the brush upright and using light pressure, flick the brush to apply short, overlapping strokes that fill up the appropriate area (do not leave empty spaces).

WET-ON-WET BLENDING: This means exactly what the name implies, applying each new colour without waiting for the previous one to dry. Work a small area at a time. This technique blends the colours together and eliminates hard edges.

Ducklings with Vegetables
Plaque
Colour Photo on Page 4

PALETTE
JO SONJA'S ARTISTS' COLOURS
Cadmium Yellow Mid
Carbon Black
Gold Oxide
Hookers Green
Indian Yellow
Nimbus Grey
Olive Green
Pacific Blue
Paynes Grey
Purple Madder
Raw Sienna
Raw Umber
Red Earth
Turners Yellow
Warm White
Yellow Oxide

BRUSHES
Angled Shader: 1/2"
Filbert: #6
Flat: #4, 1"
Liner: #10/0
Rake: 1/4"
Round: #3

PREPARATION
Remove the clothes hooks. Refer to Wood Preparation at the front of the book. Basecoat with thinned Raw Sienna. Allow to dry, then transfer the pattern omitting the duckling in front of the jug for now.

PROCEDURE
Refer to the colour worksheet to paint the ducklings, daisies and pumpkins.

BLUE JUG: Basecoat the body of the jug by slip-slapping with Pacific Blue using the #6 filbert brush. While wet, mix Pacific Blue + Warm White (1: touch) and slip-slap this on the middle of the jug with the #4 flat brush. Add more Warm White to the mix and slip-slap on the right side of the jug; add more Warm White to the dirty brush for lightest highlights. Let dry.

Use the angled shader to float thinned Paynes Grey down the left side of the jug to form a shadow. When dry, darken the shading randomly with thinned Purple Madder. Use the #4 flat brush to slip-slap a small amount of tinted Indian Yellow on the right side of the jug, above the duckling's back.

Use the #3 round brush to basecoat the handle with Pacific Blue. Use tinted Pacific Blue to highlight the right side. Float Paynes Grey with the angled shader down the left side of the handle to shade.

DAISIES: Basecoat the petals with Nimbus Grey using the #3 round brush. Use the liner brush and Warm White to highlight; the upper petals have the strongest highlights. Outline the petals with Raw Umber.

Use the liner brush to basecoat the centres with Gold Oxide, then dab over the top with Yellow Oxide. Highlight further by dabbing a little Cadmium Yellow Mid. Shade the base of the petals around the centres with thinned Paynes Grey, using the #3 round brush. Paint the stems with Hookers Green.

Use the liner brush and thinned Paynes Grey to paint the cast shadows of the petals on the jug.

BLUE FLOWERS: The blue flowers are painted freehand. Load the #3 round brush with Pacific Blue, tip into Warm White, then dab on the surface to form the flowers. Use the liner brush to paint the stems with Hookers Green.

PUMPKINS: Refer to the colour photo for colour placement. Basecoat with Gold Oxide using the #6 filbert brush.

Drybrush Turners Yellow + Gold Oxide (1:1) over the pumpkins, then drybrush Cadmium Orange.

Use full-strength, tinted Indian Yellow and the #3 round brush to paint highlights.

Mix Purple Madder + Raw Umber (1: touch) and thin to an inky consistency. Use this mix and the #6 filbert brush to shade the small pumpkin. Use the liner brush to paint a few highlights of Warm White.

Use the liner brush to add markings with Cadmium Yellow Mid on the larger pumpkin. When dry, glaze the left side of each section with Olive Green using the filbert brush. Allow this glaze to dry, then glaze with Purple Madder + Raw Umber (1: touch). Highlight with Warm White.

Basecoat the stems with Raw Umber using the liner brush. Use tinted Raw Umber and the liner brush to highlight. Use Warm White as the final highlight.

SHALLOTS: Basecoat the green areas of the shallots with Hookers Green, using the #6 filbert brush. Mix Indian Yellow + Hookers Green (1:1) and then tint the mix with Warm White; drybrush highlights on the green areas. Use this colour to basecoat the light tip of each shallot. Add more Warm White

(Continued on Page 8)

Ducklings with Vegetables

Ducklings with Vegetables
(Continued from Page 7)

to the mix and drybrush this over the lighter areas; paint Warm White on the tips. Paint a little Cadmium Yellow Mid over the green areas of a few shallots in the middle.

Shade the lower edge of the shallots with thinned Raw Umber using the #3 round brush. Use the liner brush and Hookers Green to paint the lines running down the shallots. The roots at the tips are painted with the liner brush using the following colours: Raw Umber, tinted Raw Umber, Carbon Black and Warm White.

GOURD: Basecoat the gourd with Olive Green using the #4 flat brush. Using the angled shader, drybrush Raw Sienna on the right side of the gourd to highlight. Pick up Warm White with the dirty brush and drybrush the lightest highlights.

Use the #3 round brush to drybrush Red Earth near the shallots. The markings on the gourd are painted with thinned, tinted Indian Yellow. When dry, use the liner and full-strength tinted Indian Yellow to highlight the markings.

Basecoat the stem with the liner brush and Raw Umber. Highlight with tinted Raw Umber, then with Warm White.

DUCKLINGS: Transfer the pattern for the duckling in front of the jug. Basecoat the ducklings with Raw Sienna using the #6 filbert brush. Use the angled shader and Raw Umber to float shading around the outer edge of birds.

Use the rake brush and small overlapping strokes of Turners Yellow to paint the feathers on each duckling; avoid the shadow areas. Tint Turners Yellow and paint a second layer of feathers. Paint a small amount of Purple Madder on the darkest areas of each duckling to form shadows. Continue using the rake brush and paint the lightest areas on each duckling with Warm White. Use thinned Raw Sienna and the rake brush to add feathers to deepen the colour in the darker areas. When dry, deepen the colour in some areas with Indian Yellow feathers, avoiding the areas painted with Warm White.

Basecoat the beaks with Raw Sienna using the #3 round brush. Use the liner brush and Indian Yellow to highlight. Use tinted Indian Yellow to increase the highlights. The nostrils are painted with Raw Umber. Paint a few highlights on beaks with Warm White using the liner brush. Basecoat the tongue with tinted Purple Madder using the #3 round brush. Use thinned Purple Madder and the liner brush to paint the shadow on the tongue. Shade the back of the throat with Carbon Black.

Use Raw Umber and the liner brush to paint the shape of the eyes. Paint the pupils with Carbon Black; add a highlight dot and outline the eyes with Warm White.

Basecoat the legs and feet, including webs, with Gold Oxide using the #3 round brush. Use the liner brush to highlight with Indian Yellow. Add a further highlight with Warm White. Use the angled shader to float Raw Umber shading to form the "toes." Paint tiny talons with Warm White.

SHADOWS: Float the cast shadows on the ground with the angled shader brush and thinned Raw Umber. Narrowly intensify the shadows under the pumpkins and shallots with Carbon Black. Float shading with Raw Umber along the left sides of the design elements.

FINISHING DETAILS: Use the 1" flat brush to paint the routed edges with thinned Burnt Umber. When dry, use sandpaper to lightly sand the surface, creating a distressed look.

FINISHING
Refer to "Finishing" in the General Instructions at the front of the book. Attach the clothes hooks.

Chicken Coop
Cupboard
Colour Photo on Front Cover

We had the pleasure of looking after the school chickens over the Christmas holidays. The adult chicken at the bottom is appropriately named Cuddles. Our chicken Helen is getting ready to lay an egg above her.

PALETTE
JO SONJA'S ARTISTS' COLOURS
Burnt Sienna
Burnt Umber
Cadmium Scarlet
Cadmium Yellow Mid
Carbon Black
Fawn
Gold Oxide
Naples Yellow Hue
Napthol Crimson
Nimbus Grey
Olive Green
Paynes Grey
Raw Sienna
Raw Umber
Red Earth
Warm White
Yellow Oxide

BRUSHES
Angled Shader: 1/2"
Filbert: #6
Flat: 1"
Liner: #10/0
Round: #3
Smudge Tint: #4, #8

PREPARATION

Refer to Wood Preparation at the front of the book. Basecoat the design area with Raw Sienna. Basecoat the rest of the cupboard with slightly thinned Burnt Umber. Allow to dry, sand lightly, then transfer the wooden coop structure, omitting the chickens and feeder at this stage.

PROCEDURE

Refer to the colour worksheet to paint "Cuddles" and chicks.

COOP: Using the 1" flat brush, basecoat the back of the coop (behind the chickens) with a few coats of thinned Raw Umber. When dry, use the #8 smudge tint brush to scumble some areas with Fawn, Burnt Umber and tinted Olive Green. I concentrated the green around Helen, the chicken at the top. Leave the basecoat showing to form the corners of the coop; you can float them back in with Raw Umber, if necessary.

The side walls are basecoated with Burnt Umber. Use a tint of Burnt Umber and the #4 smudge tint brush to scumble highlights.

The vertical front edges are basecoated with tinted Raw Sienna using the #3 round brush. Use the liner brush to paint wood grain with thinned Burnt Umber, then drybrush a small amount of Warm White.

The crosspieces are basecoated with Burnt Umber. Use the #3 round brush to paint streaks of tinted Raw Sienna in a horizontal direction. Leave Burnt Umber showing to form the pattern of the grain of the wood. Tint Raw Sienna further to increase the highlights.

The nails are painted using the liner brush and Burnt Umber. Tint Burnt Umber to highlight.

FEEDER: Transfer the feeder. Use the #8 filbert brush to basecoat the feeder with tinted Paynes Grey. Tint the Paynes Grey further and use the #8 smudge tint brush to scumble a highlight down the centre of the feeder. Use the dirty brush to scumble Warm White on this area to increase the highlight. Scumble a few areas with tinted Gold Oxide here and there, then follow with tinted Olive Green.

Use the #3 round brush to paint the two ridges across the centre of the feeder with tinted Paynes Grey. Use the angled shader to float Paynes Grey shading to form the edge of the lid, above and below the two ridges, and below the saucer rim. The inside left section of saucer is glazed with a slightly darker tint of Paynes Grey. Highlight the top, edge of the lid, two ridges and rim of the saucer with Warm White.

Use the #3 round brush to dab Yellow Oxide for the chicken feed; dab Naples Yellow Hue to highlight.

STRAW: Use the #3 round brush and thinned paint for the straw. Flick brush strokes with Burnt Sienna, Yellow Oxide, Naples Yellow Hue and Warm White.

HELEN (CHICKEN AT TOP): Transfer the chickens and chicks, omitting feather detail. Use the #6 filbert brush to basecoat Helen with Burnt Sienna. Allow to dry, then transfer the feather details. Use the #4 smudge tint brush to scumble Burnt Umber on her breast area, neck and upper back.

BREAST FEATHERS: Paint the feathers on her breast using the #6 filbert brush and Raw Sienna + Burnt Sienna (1:1). Dab the paint onto the surface, allowing the shape of the brush to form the feather. Define and highlight these feathers using either the #3 round brush or the liner brush and Naples Yellow Hue; add a touch of Gold Oxide here and there. Scumble tinted Burnt Sienna over this area.

WING FEATHERS: The top stray feather and the two below it are basecoated with a very light tint of Paynes Grey; use the liner brush and Warm White to add detail and highlights to these feathers. Use the #3 round brush to basecoat the remaining wing feathers with Naples Yellow Hue. Use the liner brush and Burnt Sienna to define and add markings these feathers.

NECK FEATHERS: Use the #3 round brush and Gold Oxide to paint long, thin neck feathers. Paint a few Red Earth feathers here and there. Add the lower feathers with Naples Yellow Hue. Paint the feathers on top of the head with Burnt Umber.

Use the #4 smudge tint brush to scumble Gold Oxide over the area between her neck and tail feathers, and above her wing feathers. When dry, scumble Naples Yellow Hue over this area.

LOWER BACK FEATHERS: Use the #6 filbert brush to paint the feathers above her tail feathers with Raw Sienna + Burnt Sienna (1:1). Use the liner brush to define them by lightly brushing with Naples Yellow Hue, leaving a central vein of the basecoat showing through.

TAIL FEATHERS: Use the #3 round brush to basecoat the tail feathers. The top two are painted like the grey wing feathers. The other feathers are basecoated with Raw Sienna + Burnt Sienna (1:1), then highlighted by painting over them with Naples Yellow Hue, followed by Warm White. Leave a central vein showing down the middle of some of them.

BOTTOM FEATHERS: Paint the feathers around her bottom by flicking strokes of Naples Yellow Hue, then Warm White, using the #3 round brush.

HEAD: Use the #3 round brush to basecoat the comb, wattle and area around the eye with Napthol Crimson. Highlight with Cadmium Scarlet using the same brush. Highlight further with a light tint of Cadmium Scarlet, then with a few small patches of Warm White here and there.

Use the liner brush to paint the eye. Basecoat the shape of the eye with Gold Oxide. The pupil is Carbon Black, highlighted with a tiny dot of Warm White. Outline the eye with Carbon Black + Warm White, mixed to a light grey.

Use the liner brush to paint the beak with Raw Sienna. Separate the sections with a stroke of Burnt Sienna. Highlight the beak with Warm White.

CUDDLES (CHICKEN AT BOTTOM): Use the #6 filbert brush to basecoat Cuddles with Burnt Sienna. When dry, transfer feather detail. Use the #4 smudge tint brush to scumble Burnt Umber over her neck, on her back above her wing, on her wing and on her belly in front of her legs.

(Continued on Page 10)

Chicken Coop
(Continued from Page 9)

NECK FEATHERS: Use the #3 round brush to paint the larger feathers on her neck with Gold Oxide. Use Cadmium Yellow Mid + Gold Oxide (1:1) to highlight these feathers. Apply Red Earth on some of the feathers under her wattle. The neck feathers at the back of her neck have Naples Yellow Hue highlights.

The smaller feathers on the top of her head and neck are also painted with Gold Oxide, but these are finer than the feathers lower down.

BREAST FEATHERS: Use the #6 filbert brush and Gold Oxide to form the feathers on her breast area. Just touch the brush to the surface, push and lift, letting the shape of the brush form the shape of the feather. Leaving a gap of Gold Oxide showing down the centre of each feather, use the #3 round brush or the liner brush to paint highlights with Cadmium Yellow Mid + Gold Oxide (1:1). Highlight the patch of slightly lighter feathers in the centre of the breast with a lighter tint of the highlight mix. Use the smudge tint brush and tinted Burnt Sienna to scumble non-distinct feathers starting just below her breast feathers and stretching to the beginning of her wing.

WING FEATHERS: Use the #3 round brush and tinted Burnt Sienna to basecoat the flight feathers at the end of her wing. Tint the Burnt Sienna further to highlight. Add additional highlights with Naples Yellow Hue. Use the smudge tint brush to scumble Gold Oxide, followed by tinted Burnt Sienna on the dark area of her wing. The feathers to the lower, left of wing are painted the same as the flight feathers, but have tinted Burnt Sienna scumbled over them.

BACK FEATHERS: Use the #6 filbert brush to dab Gold Oxide to form feathers on her back, above her wing. Use the liner brush to add definition around the edges of the feathers using tinted Burnt Sienna, followed by Naples Yellow Hue.

TAIL FEATHERS: Use the #3 round brush to basecoat the tail feathers with Burnt Sienna. Paint Carbon Black markings on the very end feathers. Use tinted Burnt Sienna to highlight the remaining three feathers. Outline the edges with Warm White.

FEATHERS BELOW WING: The feathers are dabbed on using the #6 filbert brush and Gold Oxide. Dab over the top of this with Cadmium Yellow Mid + Gold Oxide (1:1). Use the liner brush to paint fine feathers around her bottom and above her legs with Naples Yellow Hue, followed by Warm White.

LEGS: Use the #3 round brush to basecoat the legs with Gold Oxide. Highlight the fronts with Naples Yellow Hue. Highlight further with Warm White. The claws are painted using the liner brush and Burnt Umber. Highlight them with Warm White.

HEAD: Use the #3 round brush to basecoat the wattle, comb and area around the eye with Napthol Crimson. Highlight with Cadmium Scarlet + Cadmium Yellow Mid (1:1). Highlight further with a tint of Cadmium Scarlet. Use the liner brush to paint a tinted Burnt Sienna highlight beside her eye to indicate her ear.

(Continued on Page 13)

Chicken Coop
Centre Panel Motif

Chicken Coop
Wire Motif

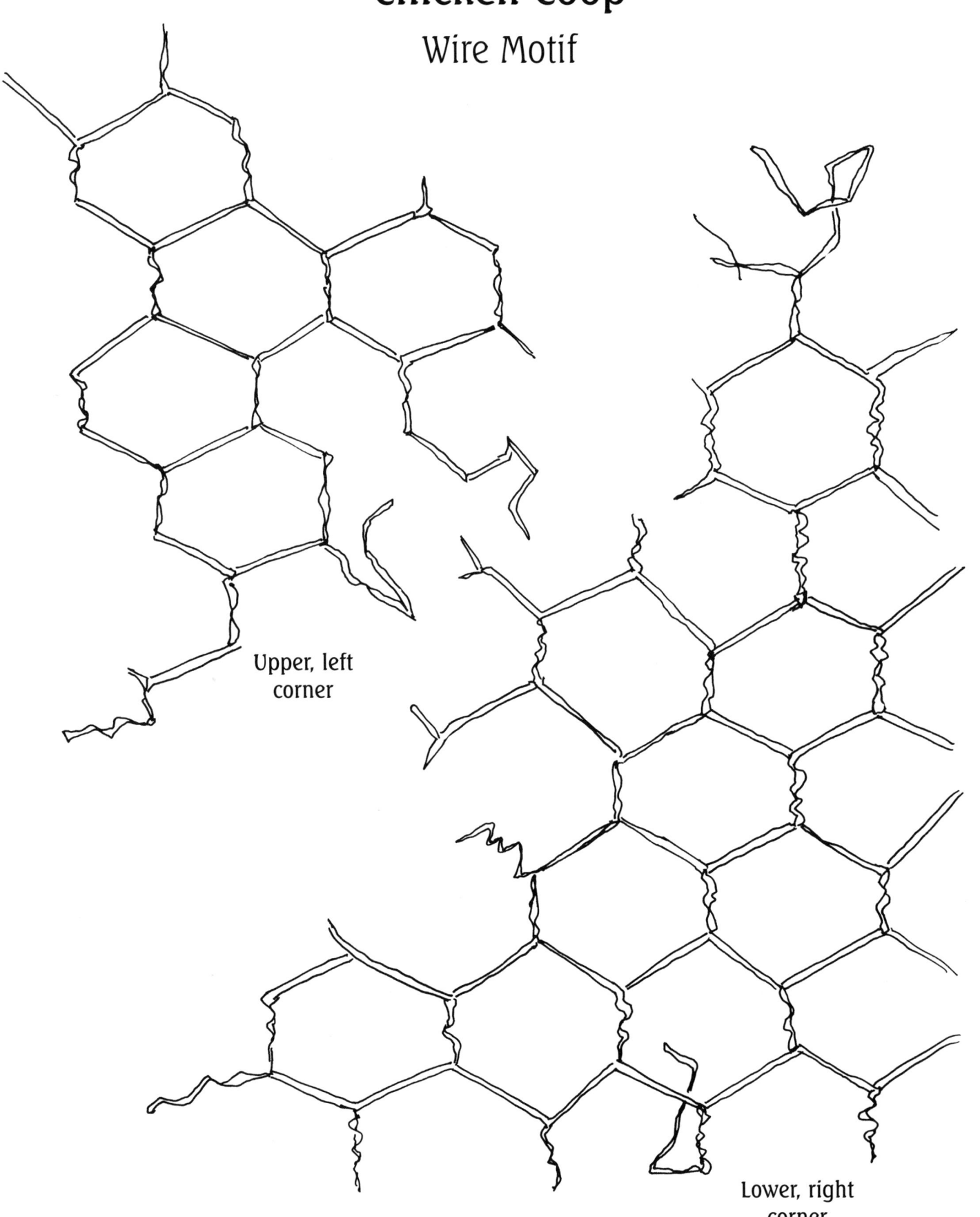

Upper, left corner

Lower, right corner

Chicken Coop
(Continued from Page 10)

Paint the eye and beak the same as Helen's. Use Burnt Umber to paint beak separations and nostril.

BABY CHICKS: Use the #6 filbert brush to basecoat the chicks with Gold Oxide. Use the #4 smudge tint brush to scumble Naples Yellow Hue on each chick, allowing the Gold Oxide to show in the darker areas to form shadows. Let dry and repeat the Naples Yellow Hue. Scumble Warm White in the lightest areas. Use the liner brush to add fine feathers around the edges with Warm White.

Use the liner brush to basecoat the eyes with Carbon Black. Using Warm White, outline each eye, then paint highlights. The beaks are basecoated with Raw Sienna and highlighted with Warm White.

The legs and feet are painted with the #3 round brush. Basecoat them with tinted Raw Sienna. Highlight them with a lighter tint of Raw Sienna, followed by Warm White. Outline them using the liner brush and Burnt Umber. The claws are Warm White.

CHICKEN WIRE: Transfer the chicken wire to the edges of the cupboard door. Use the #3 round brush to basecoat the wire with thinned Nimbus Grey. Use the liner brush to paint highlights here and there on the wire with Warm White. Shade the wire with Burnt Umber. Paint the cast shadows formed by the wire freehand. Thin Burnt Umber and use either the liner bush or the #3 round brush to paint the shadow to the right of the vertical strokes of wire and underneath each angled stroke.

SHADOWS: Using Burnt Umber, float shadows around Helen; Cuddles' head, legs and tail, next to the left chick and coop, and around outer edge of insert.

FINISHING
Refer to "Finishing" in the General Instructions at the front of the book.

Baby Chick with Vegetables
Colour Photo on Front Cover

PALETTE
JO SONJA'S ARTISTS' COLOURS

Burnt Umber	Paynes Grey
Cadmium Scarlet	Permanent Alizarine
Cadmium Yellow Mid	Purple Madder
Carbon Black	Raw Sienna
Gold Oxide	Raw Umber
Hookers Green	Red Earth
Indian Red Oxide	Turners Yellow
Indian Yellow	Warm White
Nimbus Grey	

BRUSHES
Angled Shader: 1/2"
Filbert: #6
Flat: #2, 1"
Liner: #10/0
Round: #3
Smudge Tint: #4

SUPPLIES
Foam brush, 2"
Jo Sonja's Gesso, White

PREPARATION
Refer to Wood Preparation at the front of the book. Basecoat the centre of the plate with white gesso. Allow to dry, then basecoat with Raw Sienna. Basecoat back with Burnt Umber, and the rim with thinned Burnt Umber. When dry, lightly sand the edges. Transfer the pattern.

PROCEDURE
KOHLRABI LEAVES: Basecoat the dark areas with Paynes Grey; these are behind and below the radishes, and behind the kohlrabi. Basecoat the lighter areas with Hookers Green. Use the smudge tint brush to scumble tinted Hookers Green on the lighter areas of the leaves to form highlights. Increase the highlights by adding more Warm White to the mix. Scumble Hookers Green on the Paynes Grey area of the leaf that is turned over; this is above and to the right of the radishes. Scumble a small amount of tinted Hookers Green here too. Veins will be painted later.

KOHLRABI: Basecoat this vegetable with Hookers Green + Indian Yellow (1:1). Tint the basecoat mix and use the #6 filbert brush to begin highlighting. Add more Warm White to the mix and scumble the lightest highlights using the smudge tint brush. Scumble a small amount of Warm White here and there. Basecoat the stems with tinted Hookers Green using the #3 round brush. Tint the Hookers Green further and highlight. Use the liner brush and a lighter tint of Hookers Green to paint the fine veins running through the leaves and to outline the leaves.

CAPSICUM (Pepper): Basecoat the capsicum with Raw Sienna. Use Purple Madder + Raw Sienna (1:1) and the #6 filbert brush to paint the shadows around the segments of the capsicum and stem area. Use the smudge tint brush to scumble Cadmium Yellow Mid on the top of the capsicum to form highlights. Do the same in a few small areas with Warm White. Basecoat the stem with Hookers Green. Drybrush highlights with Indian Yellow + Hookers Green (1:1), using the #2 flat brush. Tint the mix and strengthen the highlights. Partially outline the base of the stem with Paynes Grey.

BEANS: Basecoat the beans with Hookers Green. Use the #2 flat brush to highlight the beans with tinted Hookers Green, leaving a small line of the basecoat showing for the seam.

(Continued on Page 15)

Baby Chick with Vegetables

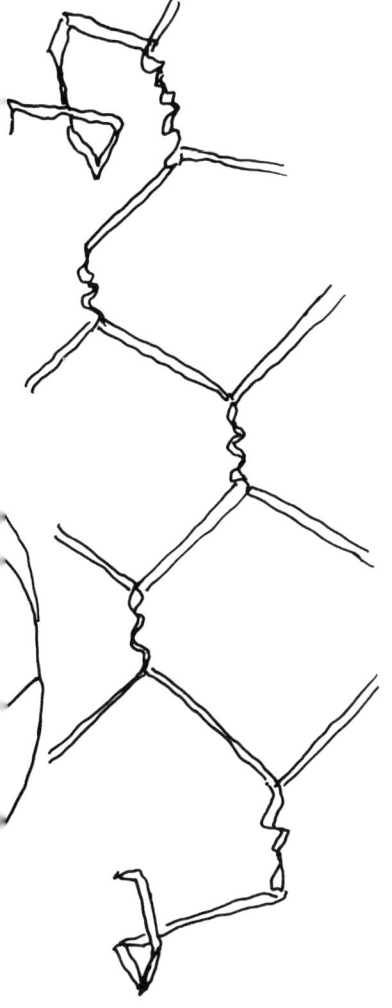

Baby Chick with Vegetables
(Continued from Page 13)

Increase the highlight by adding more Warm White to the mix. When dry, glaze Cadmium Yellow Mid over each bean with the #2 flat brush. Float Cadmium Yellow Mid on the bottom of each bean with the angled shader. Outline randomly with Paynes Grey.

RADISHES: Use the #6 filbert brush to basecoat the radishes with Permanent Alizarine. Use the smudge tint brush to scumble Cadmium Scarlet on the radishes to highlight the centre areas. Scumble Cadmium Yellow Mid + Cadmium Scarlet (1:1) to strengthen the highlights. Add final highlights with Warm White. Use the angled shader to float Indian Red Oxide to shade the edge of each radish. Use the liner brush to paint the roots with Permanent Alizarine. Highlight the roots with Cadmium Scarlet, then paint the tips with Warm White. Shade next to the chick with Paynes Grey.

CARROTS: Basecoat the carrots with Red Earth. Use the smudge tint brush to scumble Gold Oxide to begin forming highlights. Scumble Cadmium Yellow Mid + Gold Oxide (1:2) to intensify the highlights. Scumble Warm White here and there. The roots are painted with the liner brush and Warm White. The tops of the carrots are painted with the liner brush and Hookers Green; tint the Hookers Green to highlight. Shade where other elements overlap using Paynes Grey.

BABY CHICK: Refer to the colour worksheet. Basecoat the chick with Raw Sienna. Use the smudge tint brush to scumble Turners Yellow all over the chicken, but make sure you leave Raw Sienna showing to form the shadows around the wing and on the head. The scumbling may need to be repeated a few times to build up the intensity of the colour.

Basecoat the feet with tinted Raw Sienna; highlight with Warm White. Outline with thinned Burnt Umber, then paint the claws with Warm White.

Scumble Warm White on the bottom and the other light areas on the chick. The white feathers on the wing are painted with the #3 round brush and Warm White. Glaze Cadmium Yellow Mid on the yellow areas to brighten them slightly. Use the liner brush to paint fine Warm White downy feathers around the edges of the chick. Paint a few fine feathers here and there with the liner brush and Raw Umber.

The eye is painted with the liner brush. Basecoat the eye with Raw Umber. When dry, paint a Carbon Black pupil. Highlight pupil with a tiny dot of Warm White. Outline around the edge of the eye with Carbon Black + Warm White (1:4), a light grey.

Use the liner brush to basecoat the beak with Raw Sienna, then highlight with Warm White. Use Burnt Umber to paint the division line.

CHICKEN WIRE: Follow the directions for the chicken wire in the "Chicken Coop" project.

FINISHING DETAILS: Use the angled shader to float Paynes Grey shading under the baby chicken's feet, to the right of the beans, carrots and kohlrabi, and under pepper.

FINISHING

Refer to "Finishing" in the General Instructions at the front of the book.

Baby Chick with Cherries
Colour Photo on Front Cover

PALETTE
JO SONJA'S ARTISTS' COLOURS

Burnt Umber
Cadmium Scarlet
Cadmium Yellow Mid
Carbon Black
Hookers Green
Nimbus Grey
Paynes Grey
Permanent Alizarine
Raw Sienna
Raw Umber
Turners Yellow
Warm White

BRUSHES
Angled Shader: 1/2"
Filbert: #6
Flat: #2, 1"
Liner: #10/0
Round: #3
Smudge Tint: #4

SUPPLIES
Foam brush, 2"
Jo Sonja's Gesso, White

PREPARATION
Refer to Wood Preparation at the front of the book. Basecoat the centre of the plate with white gesso. Allow to dry, then basecoat with Raw Sienna. Basecoat the back with Burnt Umber, and the rim with thinned Burnt Umber. When dry, lightly sand the edges. Transfer the pattern.

PROCEDURE
COLANDER: Basecoat the colander with Paynes Grey + Warm White (1:2), using the #6 filbert brush. Use the smudge tint brush to scumble a lighter tint of Paynes Grey on the left side of the colander and under handle for highlights. Scumble Warm White for the final highlights.

Paint shadows under the rim, near and inside the handle, on the handle, on bottom of colander and on the base with thinned Paynes Grey. Scumble a small amount of tinted Permanent Alizarine on the colander to reflect the colour of the cherries. Highlight the handle and the base with thinned Warm White.

Paint the top and lower rims with Paynes Grey. Use the liner brush to highlight with tinted Paynes Grey. Use the liner brush to paint the holes in the colander with Paynes Grey. Highlight the right side of each hole with tinted Paynes Grey.

CHERRIES: Basecoat the cherries with Permanent Alizarine. Use the smudge tint brush to scumble Cadmium Scarlet on each cherry to create the round form. Make sure you leave Permanent Alizarine showing in the dimple around the stem and on shadow areas of each cherry. Tint Cadmium Scarlet with a small amount of Warm White and then thin with water. Use this colour and the #3 round brush to paint highlights on cherries. Follow this with Warm White, first thinned and then full strength. Vary the highlights for lighter and darker cherries.

Use the liner brush to basecoat the stems with tinted Hookers Green. Tint the colour further, then highlight by painting a small line on each stem. Paint a little Burnt Umber tip on each one and then highlight the tip with tinted Burnt Umber.

GREEN TOMATO: Basecoat the tomato with Hookers Green. Use Cadmium Yellow Mid + Hookers Green (1:1) and the filbert brush to highlight the tomato, leaving the basecoat showing to form the darkest shadows. Use Cadmium Yellow Mid + Hookers Green + Warm White (1:1:1) to highlight further.

RED TOMATO: Basecoat the tomato with Permanent Alizarine. To highlight, use the same technique used to highlight the cherries. Use Cadmium Scarlet to highlight. Follow this with Cadmium Scarlet + Cadmium Yellow Mid (1:1). Use the smudge tint brush to scumble a Warm White highlight on the left side. Basecoat the stem with Hookers Green; use the liner brush to highlight with tinted Hookers Green.

TOMATO LEAVES: Basecoat the leaves near tomatoes with Hookers Green. Use the small flat brush to drybrush tinted Hookers Green, pulling in from the edges toward the centre. Increase the highlight by adding more Warm White to the mix and pulling the lighter colour over the top of the darker colour. Paint the vein down the middle with tinted Hookers Green. Basecoat the stems (except the one below the chick) with Burnt Umber and highlight with tinted Burnt Umber.

The leaf and stem below the chick are basecoated with Hookers Green, then highlighted with tinted Hookers Green. If the leaves need additional shading, float Paynes Grey.

CHICK: Refer to the colour worksheet. Paint the chick the same as the one in the "Chick with Vegetable" project.

STRAW: Use the #3 round brush or the liner brush to paint the straw. Thin the paint slightly before applying. Use Burnt Umber, Turners Yellow and tinted Turners Yellow.

CHICKEN WIRE: Follow the directions for chicken wire in the "Chicken Coop" project.

FINISHING DETAILS: Use the angled shader to float Paynes Grey to the right of the chick's legs and on the cherries where a shadow is cast from one sitting in front of another. Also shade next to chick's back and head, next to cherry on bottom left and right cherry on rim, on tomato next to cherry and on background next to cherries in colander. Use a liner brush and Warm White to add a few final feathers to the chick over the shading.

FINISHING
Refer to "Finishing" in the General Instructions at the front of the book.

Baby Chick with Cherries

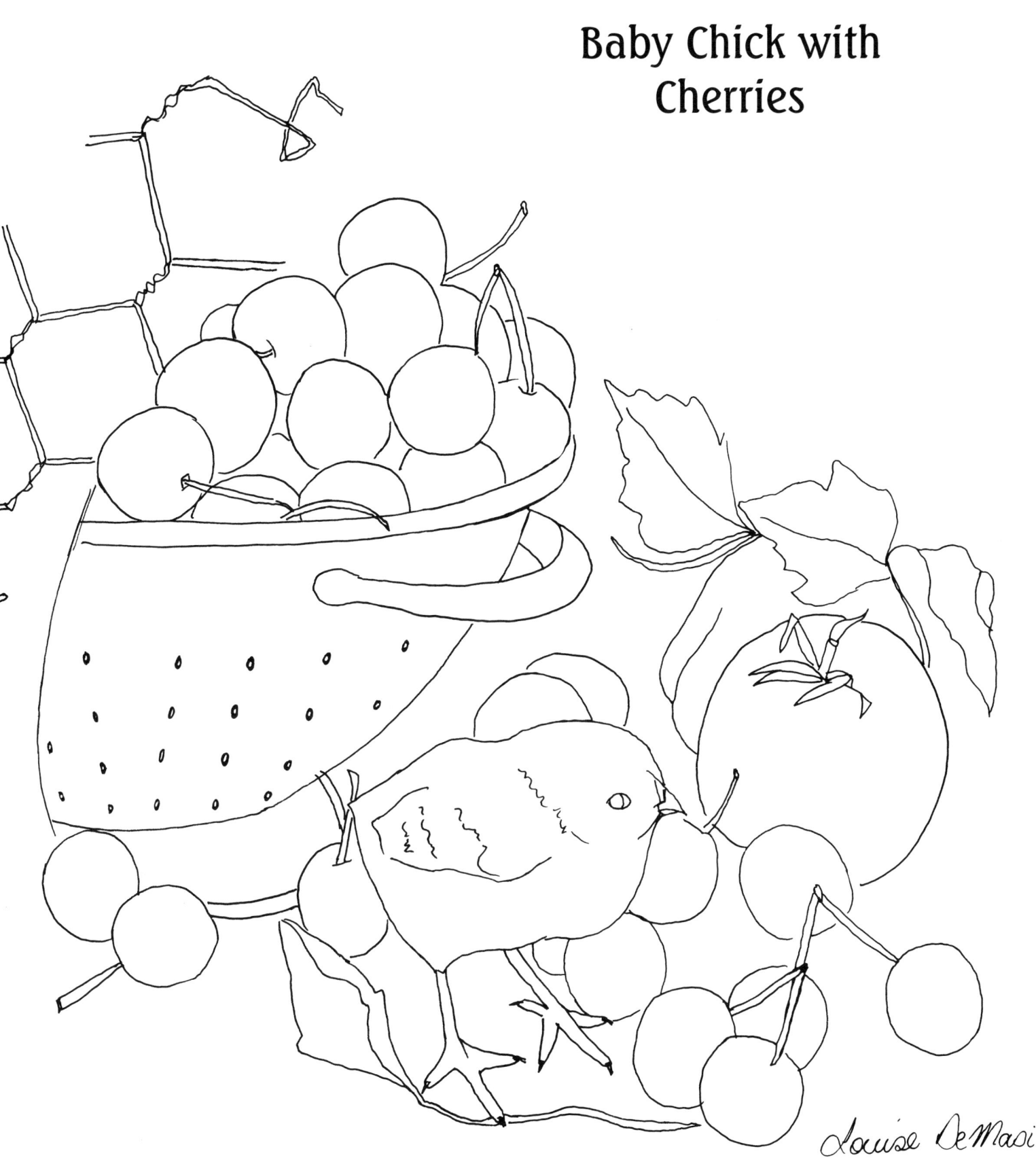

Country Kitchen Blackboard

Colour Photo on Page 23

PALETTE

JO SONJA'S ARTISTS' COLOURS
Brilliant Green
Burnt Sienna
Burnt Umber
Cadmium Scarlet
Cadmium Yellow Mid
Carbon Black
Fawn
French Blue
Gold Oxide
Moss Green
Naples Yellow Hue
Napthol Crimson
Nimbus Grey
Olive Green
Paynes Grey
Pine Green
Purple Madder
Raw Sienna
Raw Umber
Red Earth
Smoked Pearl
Titanium White
Warm White
Yellow Deep
Yellow Oxide

MATISSE ARTISTS' COLOURS
Skintone Light

BRUSHES

Angled Shader: 1/2"
Deerfoot: #4
Filbert: #6
Flat: #4, 1"
Liner: #10/0
Rake: 1/4"
Rekab Series 337 Round: #4
Round: #3, #10
Smudge Tint: #4

SUPPLIES

Foam brush, 2"
Jo Sonja's Gesso, Black

PREPARATION

Refer to Wood Preparation at the front of the book to prepare the craftwood insert and the pine frame.

Basecoat the insert with black gesso using the foam brush; you'll probably need three coats for good coverage. Allow to dry, then transfer the pattern, omitting basket weave and checks on jelly jar covering.

Use the 1" flat brush to basecoat the frame with a few coats of thinned Burnt Umber. When dry, use sandpaper to lightly sand the frame to give it a distressed finish. Transfer the patterns.

PROCEDURE

Refer to the colour worksheet to paint the pumpkin, red apple and wheat. Use Titanium White for tinting colours.

Blackboard

PITCHER: The pitcher is painted with the #4 flat brush unless otherwise indicated. Basecoat the inside of the pitcher with Nimbus Grey. Use thinned Paynes Grey and the #3 round brush to paint the cast shadows to the right sides of the utensils.

Basecoat the top section of the outside of the pitcher with Smoked Pearl and the bottom section with French Blue + Smoked Pearl (1: touch). Use as many coats as needed to achieve opaque coverage. (Handle will be painted later.)

Apply a glaze of Naples Yellow Hue on the top section. When dry, use Paynes Grey + Naples Yellow Hue (1:1) to shade the right side of the pitcher, starting at the edge and pulling the colour toward the middle, following the shape of the pitcher. Highlight the left side of the pitcher with thinned Titanium White.

On the bottom section of the pitcher, use Paynes Grey + French Blue (1:1) to shade the right side, starting at the edge and pulling the colour toward the middle. Use a tint of French Blue to highlight the left side, applying the colour on the edge and pulling it toward the middle.

Thin Paynes Grey and use the #10 round brush to apply colour to some areas on the right side of the pitcher. The pattern near the rim of the pitcher is painted with the liner brush and Raw Umber. Outline the top edge of the pitcher with Titanium White, using the #3 round brush.

Basecoat the handle with Paynes Grey using the large round brush. Add highlights with tints of Paynes Grey using the #3 round brush. The strongest highlights are Titanium White.

Drybrush a little Red Earth on the light area of the pitcher for reflected colour.

ROLLING PIN: Basecoat the rolling pin with Fawn using the #4 flat brush. Use the #10 round brush and thinned Paynes Grey to shade the right side and form the ridge at the handle. Use the same brush to drybrush Titanium White to highlight the left side.

Use the angled shader to float Raw Umber to form the wood grain. Add more detail to the wood grain using the liner brush and Raw Umber.

WOODEN SPOONS: Basecoat the wooden spoons with Smoked Pearl using the #4 flat brush. When dry, paint with Raw Sienna. Use enough coats for good coverage.

SPOON ON LEFT: Using Paynes Grey + Raw Sienna (1:1) and the #3 round brush, shade the right side and front of handle. Brush Burnt Sienna on the left side of this spoon. Use the #3 round brush to highlight the dish area with Naples Yellow Hue. Use the liner brush to paint wood grain with Raw Umber. Define the edge of the spoon with the #3 round brush and tinted Raw Sienna. Strengthen highlight with Titanium White.

SPOON ON RIGHT: Using the angled shader, float Paynes Grey just in from the left edge to form the dish of the spoon. Use the #3 round brush and thinned Raw Umber to darken the dish area. Paint wood grain in the dish area with the liner brush and Raw Umber. Define the edge of the spoon and highlight the same as the other spoon.

Float Paynes Grey with the angled shader to form a shadow along the inside front edge of the pitcher.

EGG BASKET: Basecoat the basket with Burnt Umber using the #4 flat brush. Allow to dry, then transfer the pattern for the weave. Use tinted Burnt Umber and the #3 round brush to paint the vertical sections of the basket. Streak the colour to add texture, and leave some of the basecoat showing to separate the sections. Do the same on the horizontal sections, feathering the edges where they meet the vertical sections.

Add more Titanium White to the mix to highlight the centres of the weave. When dry, randomly apply a glaze of Yellow Deep over the basket with the #4 flat brush. When dry, apply a glaze of Burnt Umber over the right side for the shadow.

EGGS: Basecoat the eggs opaquely with tinted Raw Sienna using the #6 filbert brush. Tint the Raw Sienna further and brush this over the eggs to highlight. Drybrush Titanium White with the #6 filbert brush on the left side of each egg. Using the angled shader, float Paynes Grey to shade the right edge of each egg, the eggs next to the rim of the basket, and to form shadows on eggs cast by other eggs.

PUMPKIN: Basecoat the pumpkin with Gold Oxide using the #4 flat brush. Use Paynes Grey + Gold Oxide (1:1) and the #6 filbert brush to paint the darkest areas and shadows on the pumpkin. Use full-strength Raw Umber + Purple Madder (1:1) and the filbert brush to paint the purple markings. Use the filbert brush to drybrush Yellow Deep on the left side of the sections to highlight. Pick up Titanium White with the dirty brush and add stronger highlights.

Basecoat the stem with Raw Umber using the #3 round brush. Use tinted Raw Umber to highlight the stem. Use the liner brush to highlight with Titanium White.

GREEN APPLES: Basecoat the apples with Moss Green using the #4 flat brush. Use the filbert brush to highlight and shade. Use Olive Green + Paynes Grey (1: touch) to paint the darkest shadows on each apple. Paint streaks here and there with Brilliant Green + Moss Green (1:1). Brush Yellow Deep on the lightest areas of each apple. Use Titanium White for the final highlights. Use the liner brush to paint Raw Umber lines near the stems. Basecoat the stems with Raw Umber, then highlight with tints of Raw Umber.

RED APPLE: Basecoat the apple with Napthol Crimson using the #4 flat brush. Use the filbert brush to highlight and shade. Paint the darkest shadows on the right of the apple and in the stem area with Purple Madder + Paynes Grey (1:1). Paint streaks of Cadmium Scarlet on the middle and left side. Pick up Yellow Deep with the dirty brush, then highlight the centre of the left side and stem area. Drybrush Titanium White as the final highlight. Paint the stem the same as the those on the green apples.

MOUSE: Basecoat mouse with Nimbus Grey using the #6 filbert brush. Paint a layer of hair over the mouse using the rake brush and Warm White. Use the rake brush and Paynes Grey to paint hair in the darker areas. Highlight by painting a layer of Titanium White hair in the lightest areas.

(Continued on Page 22)

Country Kitchen Blackboard

Frame Bottom Right Corner Motif

Remaining Patterns on Pages 20-21 & 24-25

Frame Top Motif

Country Kitchen Blackboard

Instructions on Pages 18-19 & 22

Frame Bottom Left Corner Motif

Remaining Patterns on Pages 18-19 & 24-25

Country Kitchen Blackboard
(Continued from Page 19)

The tail, nose, feet and ears are basecoated with Fawn using the #3 round brush. Highlight these with Matisse's Skintone Light. Strengthen highlights with Titanium White. Shade inside the ears with Burnt Umber. Basecoat the eye with Carbon Black using the liner brush; the highlight is Titanium White. Outline with Skintone Light. The whiskers are painted with Titanium White using the liner brush.

JAR OF JAM: Basecoat the jam in the jar with Red Earth using the #4 flat brush. Allow to dry. Use thinned Yellow Deep and the large round brush to add highlights on the jam. Apply the paint fairly wet; interesting swirls of colour should appear. Use thinned Purple Madder to add darker areas under the cloth top, and here and there.

When dry, use the angled shader to float Titanium White around the edge of the jar and down the centre to form the glass. Use Titanium White and the liner brush to add bright highlights on the edges and the front of the jar.

Basecoat the cloth top on the jar with Nimbus Grey using the #4 flat brush. When dry, transfer the checks. Use thinned Napthol Crimson and the #3 round brush to paint stripes, first in one direction, then in the other direction. Use the liner brush and slightly thinned Napthol Crimson to darken the checks where the stripes intersect. Highlight the centre of the darker red checks with Cadmium Scarlet. Highlight the Nimbus Grey squares on the left side of the top with Titanium White. Float Paynes Grey shading with the angled shader along the front edge of the rim of the jar. Float Titanium White along the top edge of the rim of the jar next to the shading and along the back edge. The string is basecoated with the #3 round brush and Raw Umber; highlight with tinted Raw Umber using the liner brush.

SUNFLOWERS: Basecoat the petals with Yellow Deep using the #3 round brush. Stroke tinted Yellow Deep over the basecoat, allowing the basecoat colour to form shadows and ridges on the petals. When dry, apply a glaze of Cadmium Yellow Mid over the petals. Use the liner brush to add highlights on some of the petals with Titanium White.

Stipple the centres with Burnt Umber using the deerfoot brush. When dry, tip the toe of the dirty deerfoot brush into Red Earth and stipple the highlights on the centres. Use the #3 round brush to randomly add thinned Red Earth on the petals.

Basecoat the stems with Olive Green using the #3 round brush. Use Yellow Deep + Olive Green (1:1) and the liner brush to highlight. Basecoat the tiny leaves behind the petals and paint the tendrils using the liner brush and Olive Green; highlight the leaves with Olive Green + Yellow Deep (1:1).

FINISHING DETAILS: Use the large round brush or the #3 round brush to paint thinned Paynes Grey cast shadows on the pitcher, basket, apple and pumpkin.

Frame

LETTERING: The lettering is painted with the Rekab round brush and thinned Smoked Pearl, using as many coats as necessary to achieve coverage. Sand lightly with sandpaper when dry.

RIBBON: Basecoat the ribbon with French Blue using the #3 round brush. Using the smudge tint brush, scumble highlights on the ribbon with tinted French Blue. Also scumble a few highlights of Naples Yellow Hue. Strengthen the highlights with a lighter tint of French Blue. This lighter highlight should cover a smaller area, allowing the previous highlights to show through around the edges. Pick up Titanium White with the dirty brush and paint final, smaller highlights. Use the liner brush to define the edges of the ribbon with tinted French Blue.

SUNFLOWER LEAVES: Use the #6 filbert brush to basecoat the leaves at the top of the frame with Pine Green. Use tinted Pine Green to drybrush highlights, pulling colour from the edges and toward the centre. Lighten the mix with more Warm White and softly drybrush again. Pick up a small amount of Cadmium Yellow Mid on the dirty brush and drybrush highlights here and there. Use the liner brush and tinted Pine Green to outline the edges of the leaves and to paint the veins.

SUNFLOWERS: Stipple the centre of each flower using the deerfoot brush and Burnt Umber. Pick up Cadmium Scarlet on the dirty brush and stipple a circular highlight on each centre. Basecoat the petals with Warm White using the #3 round brush. Paint over the basecoat colour with Yellow Deep. Use tinted Yellow Deep and the #3 round brush to highlight the petals, pulling the colour from the edge of the petal toward the centre. Paint thinned Cadmium Scarlet on the petals next to the centres. Thin Burnt Umber with water and use the liner brush to pull strokes from the centre and to paint dots on the petals. Outline the petals using the liner brush and Burnt Umber.

The smaller leaves behind the petals are painted with the liner brush. Basecoat the leaves with Pine Green, then use tinted Pine Green to highlight them the same way that the sunflower petals were highlighted. Outline the leaves with tints of the same colour.

WHEAT: Basecoat the wheat and stems with Yellow Oxide using the #3 round brush. Paint a small highlight on the inner edge of each segment with tinted Yellow Oxide. Outline the wheat using the liner brush and Burnt Umber. Paint the fine wispy strokes using the liner brush and Warm White. The tendrils are painted with a tint of Yellow Oxide and Warm White.

FINISHING

Refer to "Finishing" in the General Instructions at the front of the book to varnish the frame. Use the #4 flat brush to varnish the design area of the blackboard.

Patterns on Pages 18-21 & 24-25

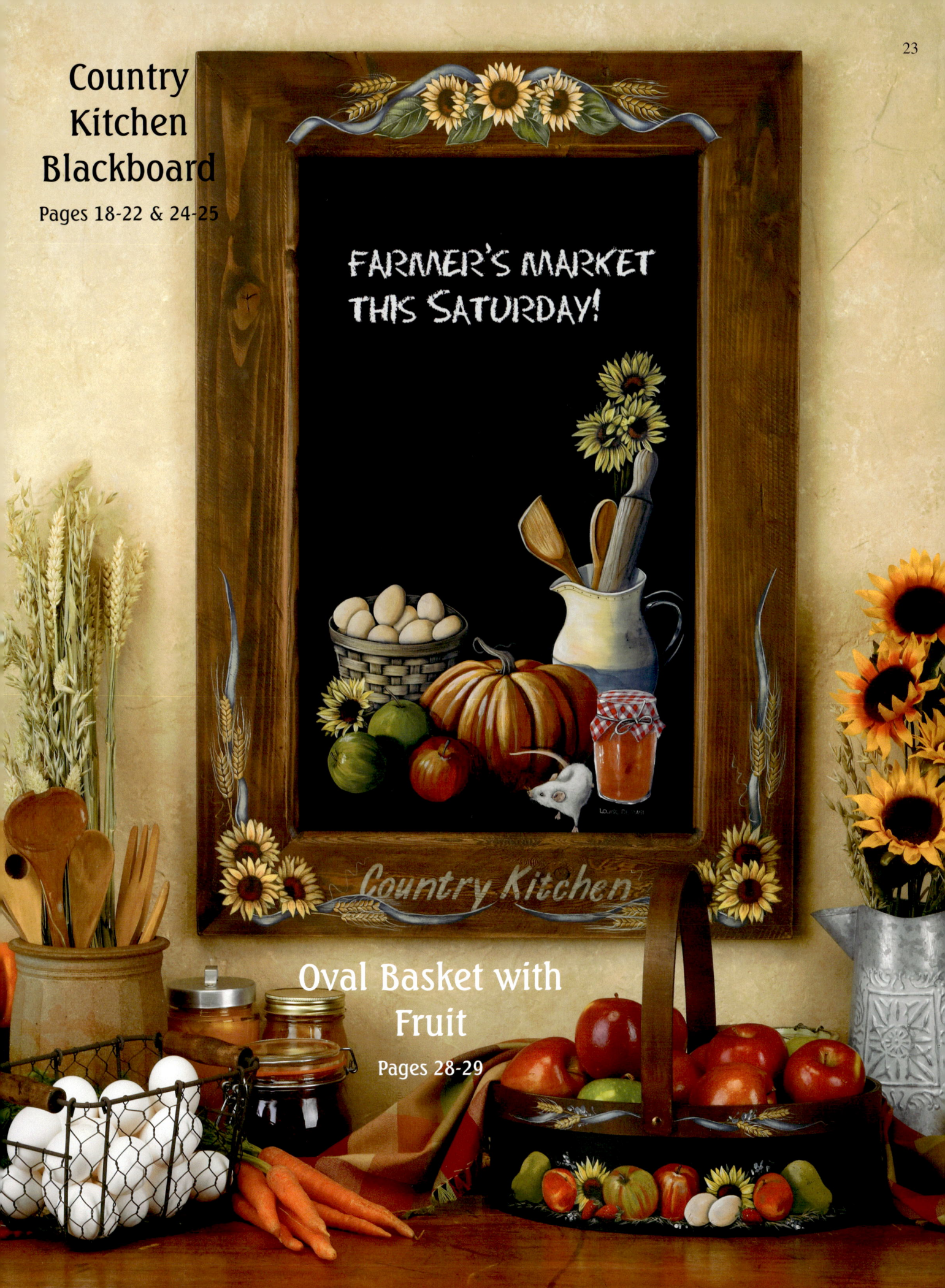

Country Kitchen Blackboard

Instructions on Pages 18-19 & 22

Blackboard Motif

Match and attach the pattern sections

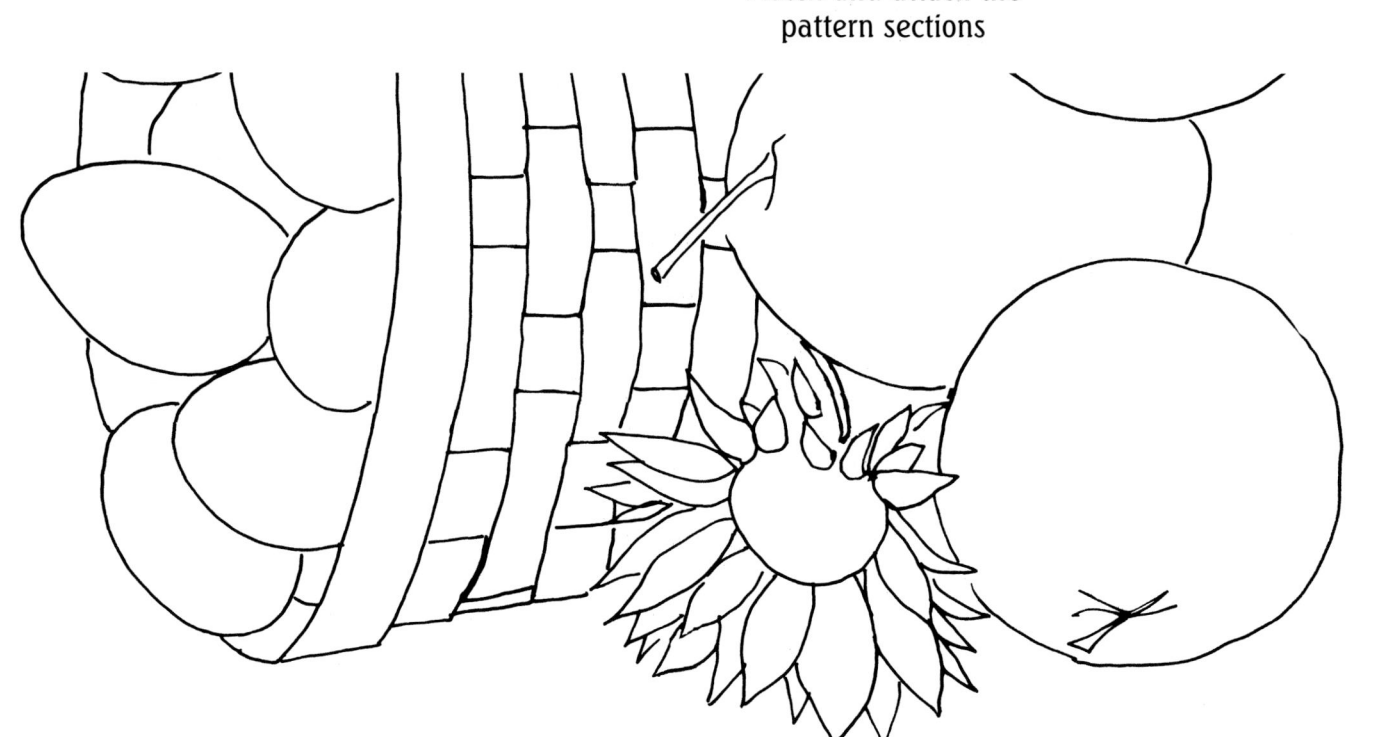

Remaining Patterns on
Pages 18-21

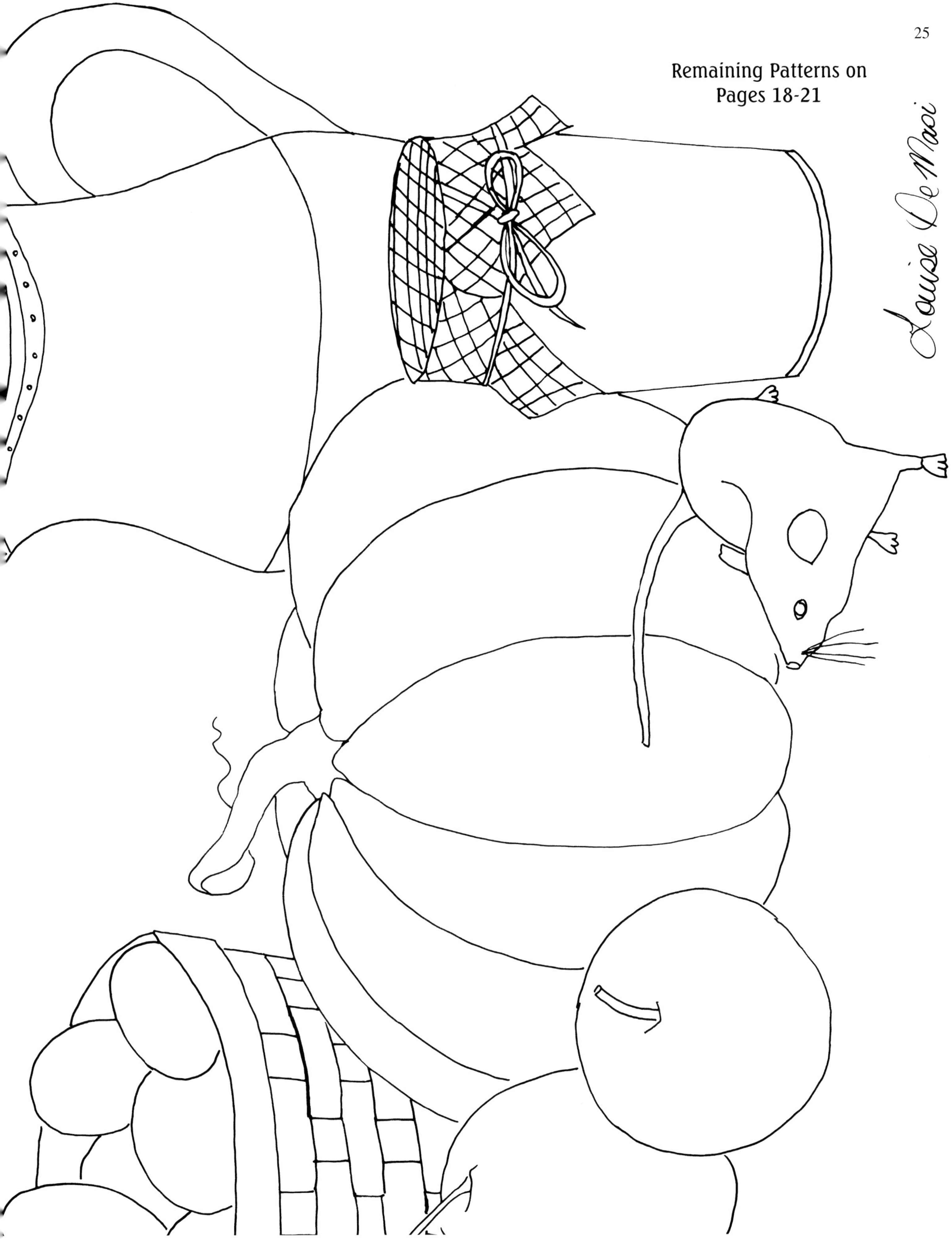

25

Louise DeMasi

Terra Cotta Pot

Daisy

Wheat

Chick

Eyes

Red Apple

Pumpkin

Eyes

Duckling

Eyes

"Cuddles"

Oval Basket with Fruit
Colour Photo on Page 23

PALETTE
JO SONJA'S ARTISTS' COLOURS

Brilliant Green	Paynes Grey
Burnt Umber	Permanent Alizarine
Cadmium Yellow Mid	Pine Green
Cadmium Scarlet	Purple Madder
French Blue	Raw Sienna
Gold Oxide	Red Earth
Hookers Green	Titanium White
Moss Green	Warm White
Napthol Crimson	Yellow Deep
Olive Green	Yellow Oxide
Pacific Blue	

BRUSHES
Angled Shader: 1/2"
Filbert: #6
Flat: #4, 1"
Liner: #10/0
Round: #3
Smudge Tint: #4

SUPPLIES
Jo Sonja's Gesso, Black
Toothbrush (for spattering)

PREPARATION
Refer to Wood Preparation at the front of the book. Basecoat the inside of the basket, the handle and the rim with thinned Burnt Umber. Basecoat the design area with black gesso. Allow to dry, then transfer the pattern.

PROCEDURE
Refer to the colour worksheet to paint the red apple and wheat. Use Titanium White for tinting colours, unless Warm White is specified.

APPLES: Basecoat the apple on the left with Moss Green using the #6 filbert brush. Paint streaks with full-strength Cadmium Scarlet following the shape of the apple to indicate roundness. Use full-strength Brilliant Green + Moss Green (1:1) to accent the green areas of the apple. Paint streaks of Gold Oxide, then highlight by drybrushing with Warm White.

Paint the stem area with Olive Green. Basecoat the stem with Burnt Umber using the liner brush; tint Burnt Umber to highlight.

The apple on the right is painted the same as the red apple on the "Country Kitchen Blackboard" project; please refer to colour photo for colour placement. Paint the stem area Olive Green.

SUNFLOWERS AND EGGS: Follow the directions in the "Country Kitchen Blackboard" project. Follow the instructions for the sunflowers on the blackboard, but don't add Red Earth to the petals. Outline petals with thinned Burnt Umber.

Basecoat the small green leaves with Hookers Green, then highlight with a tint of Hookers Green.

STRAWBERRIES: Basecoat the strawberries using Permanent Alizarine and the #3 round brush. Use the smudge tint brush to scumble Cadmium Scarlet, then paint a few Warm White highlight strokes on the upper side of each strawberry.

Use the liner brush to paint the seeds with Burnt Umber. Highlight each seed with a small dot of Yellow Oxide. Use the #3 round brush and Hookers Green to basecoat the calyxes. Use tinted Hookers Green to highlight; tint the Hookers Green further and use the liner brush to randomly outline each leaf.

PEARS: Basecoat the pears with Moss Green using the #6 filbert brush. Use Pine Green + Moss Green (1:1) to paint the shadow areas. While wet, paint Moss Green near the centre of

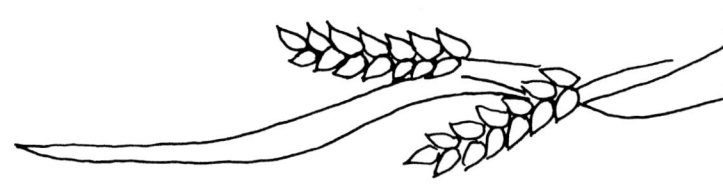

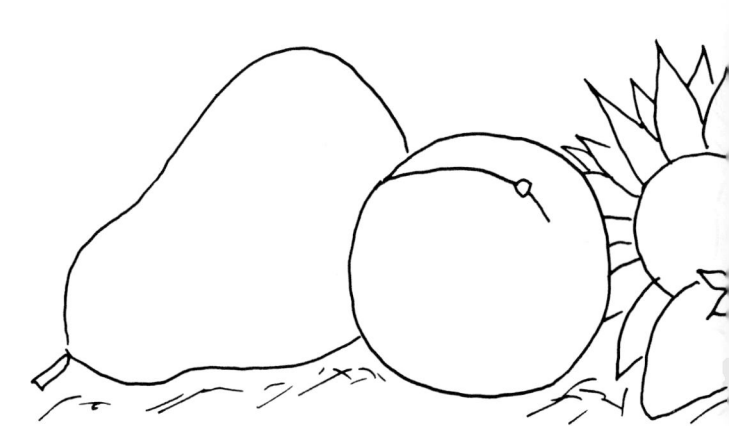

each pear to help blend the colours together. When dry, glaze Yellow Deep on the upper portion of each pear to brighten the colour. Tint Moss Green with Warm White and scumble the lightest highlights. Cover the surrounding areas, then use the old toothbrush and your thumb to flick thinned Pine Green onto the surface of each pear. Use Yellow Oxide + Burnt Umber (1:1) and the liner brush to paint the stem area. Using the liner brush, basecoat the stem with Burnt Umber; use tinted Burnt Umber to highlight.

PEACHES: Use the #6 filbert brush to basecoat the peaches with Yellow Oxide. Paint over the basecoat with Cadmium Scarlet + Napthol Crimson + Yellow Deep (1:1:1), leaving the basecoat colour showing in the indentation where the stem emerges. Shade the indentation with Burnt Umber. Use Purple Madder + Napthol Crimson (1:1) to paint the darker area near the base of each peach. The yellow markings are painted with Yellow Deep. Use the liner brush and Burnt Umber to basecoat the stems, then highlight the ends with Yellow Oxide.

STRAW: Use the #3 round brush to paint the straw with Yellow Oxide and Warm White.

RIBBON: Follow the directions for the ribbon in the "Country Kitchen Blackboard" project. Omit the yellow highlights.

BLUE FLOWERS: The blue flowers are painted freehand. Load the #3 round brush with Pacific Blue, tip into Warm White, then dab on the surface to form the flowers. Use the liner brush to paint the stems with Hookers Green.

WHEAT: Follow the directions for the wheat in the "Country Kitchen Blackboard" project.

FINISHING DETAILS: Float Paynes Grey with the angled shader to form the shadows where one piece of fruit sits in front of another.

FINISHING

Refer to "Finishing" in the General Instructions at the front of the book.

Oval Basket with Fruit

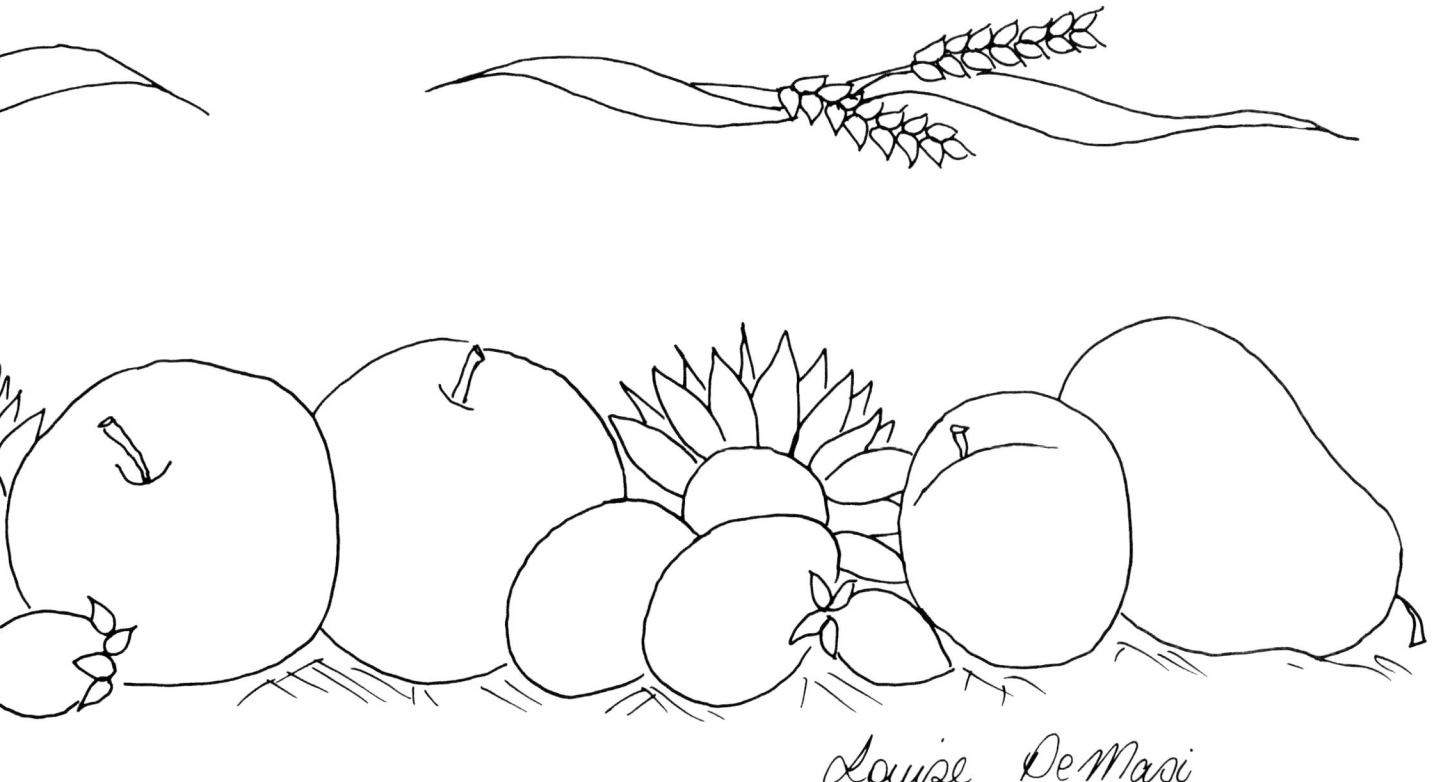

Louise DeMasi

30

Welcome to My Garden
Pages 31-37

Welcome to My Garden
Plaque with Welcome Sign
Colour Photo on Page 30

PALETTE
JO SONJA'S ARTISTS' COLOURS
Burnt Sienna
Burnt Umber
Cadmium Yellow Mid
Carbon Black
Dioxazine Purple
Gold Oxide
Hookers Green
Naples Yellow Hue
Napthol Crimson
Pacific Blue
Paynes Grey
Purple Madder
Raw Sienna
Red Earth
Turners Yellow
Warm White
Yellow Oxide

BRUSHES
Angled Shader: 1/2"
Deerfoot: #4
Filbert: #6
Flat: #2, #4, 1"
Liner: #10/0
Rekab Series 337 Round: #4
Round: #3, #10

PREPARATION
Refer to Wood Preparation at the front of the book. Basecoat both pieces with Raw Sienna. Paint the routed edges with Burnt Umber. Allow to dry, then transfer the patterns.

PROCEDURE
Refer to the colour worksheet to paint the terra cotta pots.

Plaque

BACKGROUND: Use the #10 round brush to randomly apply thinned Burnt Umber in a carefree manner on the background behind the wheelbarrow. Paint the cast shadow under the wheelbarrow the same way with thinned Paynes Grey.

WHEELBARROW: Basecoat the wooden sides and front, handles, stands, pieces holding the wheel, the spokes and hub, and the bottom half of the wheel rim with Hookers Green. Basecoat the framework holding the box and the top half of the wheel rim with Burnt Umber.

Tint Hookers Green and use the #3 round brush to drybrush highlights on the green areas. Add more Warm White for additional highlights. Drybrush highlights on the framework and left side of the top half of the wheel rim with tinted Burnt Umber; add more Warm White for additional highlights.

Float Hookers Green shading with the angled shader on the wooden sides and front next to the framework. Other shadows are the basecoat colour showing through.

MILK CAN: Basecoat the milk can with Burnt Sienna. The remaining steps may need to be repeated to blend the colours into one another. It helps if the brush isn't washed between colours. While the basecoat is still wet, use the #4 flat brush to shade the left side of the milk can with Burnt Umber + Burnt Sienna (1:1), and then pull the colour from the edge to about the middle of the milk can. While wet, blend Red Earth down the middle of the milk can. Brush Gold Oxide over the right side of the can. Use Turners Yellow to intensify the colour on the right side. The lightest highlight along the right edge is Naples Yellow Hue. Allow to dry. Use the angled shader float the shadows along the rims and edges with Burnt Umber. Use the liner brush to highlight the rims with Naples Yellow Hue. Use the liner brush to basecoat the handles with Burnt Sienna. Shade with Burnt Umber and highlight with Naples Yellow Hue. There is a little Red Earth on the handles.

POTS ON THE RIGHT: Basecoat the outside of the round terra cotta pots with Gold Oxide. The pot in the middle of this group is basecoated with Hookers Green.

Tint Hookers Green, then use the #3 round brush to drybrush highlights on the green pot; your strokes should start at the top and follow the shape of the pot as you work toward the bottom. Add more Warm White to the mix to strengthen the highlight.

Basecoat the inside wall of the round pot at the top of the pile with Burnt Umber. Use the #3 round brush and Red Earth to drybrush highlights on this area. The base of this pot, visible inside, is basecoated with Gold Oxide and highlighted with tinted Gold Oxide. The drainage hole is painted with Burnt Umber using the liner brush. Highlight the edge of the hole with Naples Yellow Hue.

Highlight outside of the rest of the pots in the pile and those inside the green pot by drybrushing with Naples Yellow Hue and tinted Gold Oxide, using the #3 round brush. Paint the insides of these pots with Burnt Umber.

The square pot on the end has two sides and the bottom visible. Basecoat the front side with Gold Oxide + Burnt Umber (1:1); highlight with tinted Gold Oxide. Basecoat the top side with Gold Oxide. Drybrush the top side with Naples Yellow Hue. Use the angled shader to float under the ridges on both sides and along edges of front side with Burnt Umber. Highlight along the ridges with the liner brush and Naples Yellow Hue. Basecoat the bottom of the pot with Gold Oxide.

(Continued on Page 32)

Welcome to My Garden
(Continued from Page 31)

Shade to form the feet using the liner brush and Burnt Umber, then highlight them with Naples Yellow Hue.

POTS IN WHEELBARROW: Basecoat with Gold Oxide. Use the #6 filbert brush to shade each pot with Burnt Umber + Gold Oxide (1:1), applying this colour along the left edge and pulling toward the middle. Highlight the right side by pulling tinted Gold Oxide from the edge. Use the angled shader to float Burnt Umber shading under the rims and inside the pots to form the shadows. Add a final highlight of Warm White on the right side of the pots.

VIOLETS IN POT: Basecoat the leaves with Hookers Green using the #3 round brush. Using the same brush and tinted Hookers Green, drybrush highlights on the leaves by applying colour near the edge of the leaf and pulling toward the middle. Add more Warm White to the mix to strengthen the highlight. Partially outline leaves and paint the veins using the liner brush and Warm White.

Basecoat the violets with tinted Dioxazine Purple using the liner brush. Add more Warm White to the mix, then highlight the petals by applying colour on the edges and pulling inward. Repeat with a slightly lighter mix. If you lose the dark colour, pull some out from the middle. Use the liner brush to outline the violets with Warm White; add the dots in the centres with Turners Yellow.

CHICKEN: Basecoat the chicken with Burnt Sienna using the #6 filbert brush. Brush Burnt Umber on the darkest areas of the chicken. To highlight and create feathers, dab tinted Burnt Sienna with a #3 round brush. Do the same with full-strength Red Earth here and there.

Welcome to My Garden
Plaque Motif

Match and attach with the pattern section on page 34

The longer feathers on the neck are painted with the liner brush and tinted Burnt Sienna. Add highlights of Warm White to the tail, back and neck. Add a few highlights of Naples Yellow.

Use the liner brush to basecoat the feet and legs with tinted Burnt Umber. Add more Warm White to the mix to highlight. Use the liner brush to partially outline with Burnt Umber.

Basecoat the comb, wattle and area around the eye with Napthol Crimson. Highlight with tinted Napthol Crimson. Use the liner brush to add tiny Turners Yellow highlights on the comb. Use the liner brush to basecoat the beak with tinted Turners Yellow; highlight with Warm White. Paint the line between sections with Burnt Umber. Basecoat the eye with Carbon Black, add a highlight dot of Warm White and outline with Turners Yellow.

POTS ON THE LEFT: Basecoat the pots with Gold Oxide. Mix Gold Oxide + Purple Madder (1:1) and use the #4 flat brush to shade the left side of each pot, pulling the colour toward the middle. Working wet-on-wet, pull highlight strokes from the right edge inward with tinted Gold Oxide. Brush some Gold Oxide down the middle of each pot to blend the shading with the highlighting. Allow to dry. Drybrush Naples Yellow Hue on the right side of each pot to strengthen the highlight. Use the angled shader to float Paynes Grey shading under each rim and inside each pot. Use the #6 filbert brush to paint thinned Paynes Grey on the left side of each pot to strengthen the shadows. Define and highlight the rims of the pots by outlining with tinted Gold Oxide, using the liner brush.

(Continued on Page 35)

Welcome to My Garden
Plaque Motif

Match and attach with the pattern
section on pages 32-33

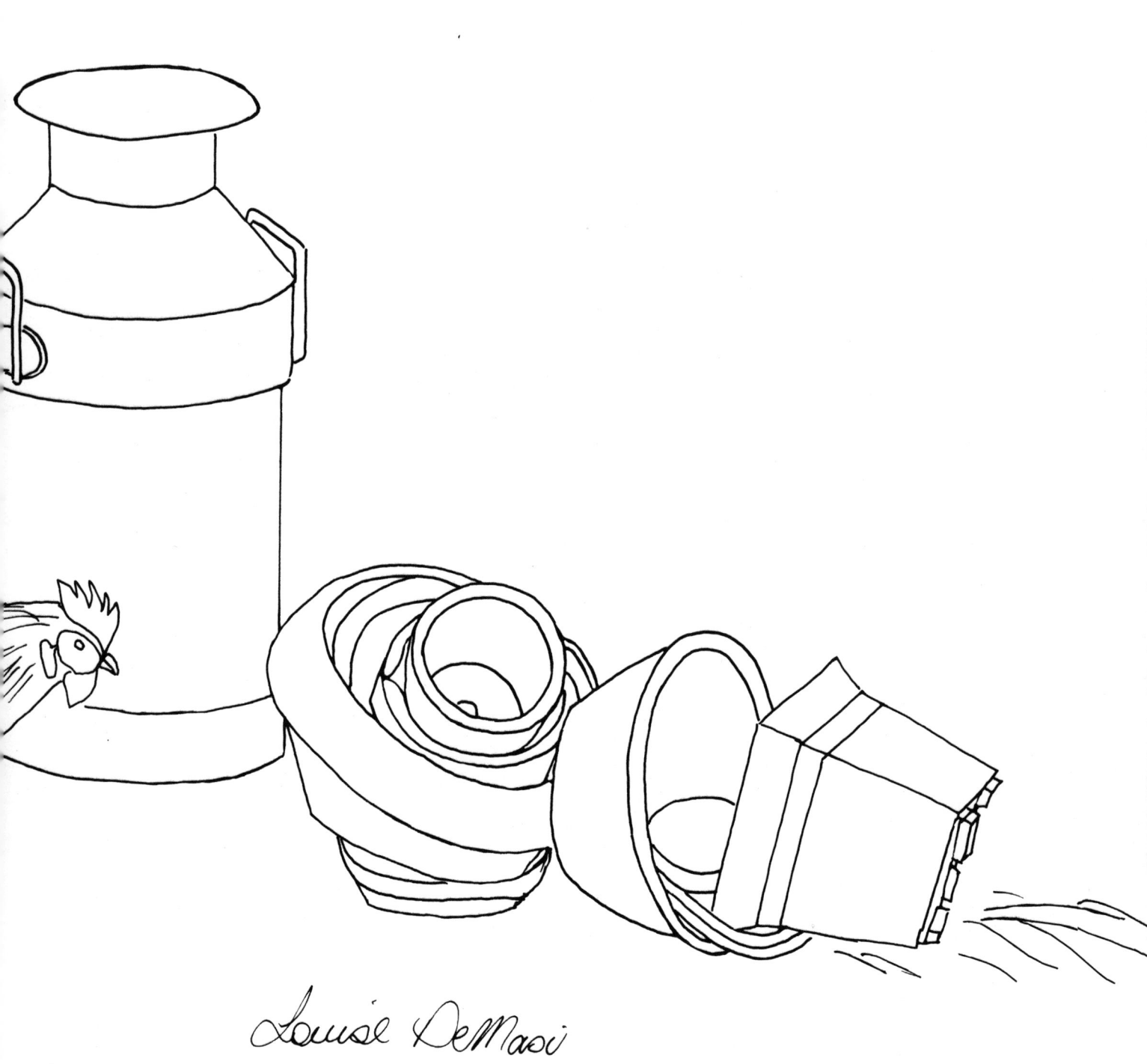

Welcome to My Garden
(Continued from Page 33)

DAFFODILS AND BLUE FLOWERS IN POT: Use the #4 deerfoot brush to stipple Burnt Umber inside the pot to form the soil. Let dry, then pick up Warm White on the toe of the dirty brush to highlight.

Use the #3 round brush and Hookers Green to paint the foliage. Mix Turners Yellow + Hookers Green (1:1) and add more foliage. Brush Turners Yellow to highlight the foliage in front.

Basecoat the daffodils with Turners Yellow using the #3 round brush. Use the liner brush to highlight each petal with tinted Turners Yellow, pulling from the tip toward the middle. Highlight the side of the trumpets in the same way, then highlight the edge of the trumpets. When dry, glaze thinned Cadmium Yellow Mid over the daffodils to brighten them. Use the liner brush and Burnt Umber to paint the dots in the throats and to outline some of the petals.

Paint the blue flowers freehand. Load the #3 round brush with Pacific Blue + Dioxazine Purple (1:1) and tip into Warm White. Press the brush to the surface to form the flowers.

STRAW: Using the #3 round brush, begin painting the straw with slightly thinned Burnt Umber. Turn the piece on its side so that you can pull each stroke toward yourself. Overlap the straw as you paint. Be patient; it takes time. Apply Red Earth next in the same manner, then follow this with Yellow Oxide. Paint the lighter straw at the front with Naples Yellow Hue.

CAST SHADOWS: Use the angled shader to float Paynes Grey to form the cast shadows.

Sign

BACKGROUND: Use the #10 round brush to randomly apply thinned Burnt Umber in a carefree manner on the background behind the pots.

POTS: Paint following the instructions for the pots on the left side of the plaque. After you've painted the straw, paint the cast shadows with thinned Paynes Grey.

LETTERING: Use the Rekab round brush to paint the lettering with thinned, tinted Yellow Oxide; you will probably need two coats. When dry, use the liner brush and thinned Burnt Umber to paint a drop shadow to the left and below each letter stroke of "Welcome." Drybrush Warm White on the thicker strokes of each of the letters with the #3 round brush.

HEN HOUSE SIGN: Basecoat boards with Burnt Umber. Use the #3 round brush and tinted Burnt Umber to drybrush highlights. Add additional Warm White to the mix and highlight the lightest edges. The basecoat will form the shading; if you've lost too much, float with Burnt Umber. Paint the lettering with the liner brush and thinned Burnt Umber. Float the cast shadow with Paynes Grey.

SPIDER'S WEB: Paint using the liner brush and thinned Warm White.

LANTERN: Basecoat the lantern (except the glass) with Paynes Grey. Use the #3 round brush or the liner brush to highlight the right side of the lantern with tinted Paynes Grey. Add additional Warm White to the mix to strengthen the highlight. Use the liner brush to paint a few highlights of Warm White.

Float Paynes Grey on the left side of the glass. When dry, float Warm White to form the shape of the glass. Use the liner brush and Warm White to add more intense highlights.

Use the liner brush and Paynes Grey to basecoat the hook. Highlight with Warm White. Paint the cast shadow with Paynes Grey.

BIRDHOUSE: Basecoat the roofs with Hookers Green and the walls with Yellow Oxide.

Use a filbert brush to drybrush tinted Yellow Oxide on the walls, then drybrush Warm White on the sides facing the light source. Use the angled shader to float Burnt Umber shading along the edges to form the corners.

Highlight each roof by drybrushing tinted Hookers Green with the #3 round brush. Use the liner brush and tinted Hookers Green to define the edges on the roof.

Basecoat the holes using the liner brush and Carbon Black. The edge of each hole is painted with tinted Burnt Umber, then highlighted with a lighter tint of Burnt Umber.

Basecoat the perches with Burnt Umber; highlight with tinted Burnt Umber.

Use the #3 round brush and thinned Paynes Grey to form the cast shadows. Paint the platform and post for the birdhouse using the colours of the sign.

STRAW: Follow the instructions for the straw on the plaque. Don't forget to paint the straw in the pot.

FINISHING

Refer to "Finishing" in the General Instructions at the front of the book.

Pattern for Sign on Pages 36-37

Welcome to My Garden

Instructions on Pages 31-33 & 35

Sign Motif

come

garden

Louise DeMasi

Cow and Calf
Bucket
Colour Photo on Back Cover

PALETTE
JO SONJA'S ARTISTS' COLOURS
Burnt Sienna
Burnt Umber
Carbon Black
Dioxazine Purple
Fawn
Naples Yellow Hue
Nimbus Grey
Olive Green
Pacific Blue
Raw Sienna
Raw Umber
Red Earth
Titanium White
Warm White
JO SONJA'S BACKGROUND COLOURS
Dolphin Blue
Primrose

BRUSHES
Angled Shader: 1/2"
Fan: #3
Filbert: #6
Flat: #4, 1"
Liner: #10/0
Rekab Series 337 Round: #4
Round: #3, #12 (or old toothbrush)

SUPPLIES
Acrylic galvanised iron primer
Jo Sonja's Retarder Medium
White vinegar

PREPARATION
The tin bucket used for this project is new. Wash the bucket with vinegar + water. Allow to dry thoroughly, then apply three coats of acrylic galvanised iron primer. When dry, apply three or four coats of Primrose on the outside of the bucket, then paint the inside with Dolphin Blue. Allow to dry, then transfer the pattern, omitting the banner.

PROCEDURE
Use Titanium White for tinting colours.

FENCE: Use the #3 round brush to basecoat the fence with Raw Umber. Apply as many coats as necessary for opaque coverage. Use tinted Raw Umber and the #3 round brush to streak highlights to form the wood grain. Add more Titanium White to the mix to highlight further. Paint a highlight along the top and left sides of the boards using the liner brush and Titanium White.

(Continued on Page 40)

Cow and Calf

Cow and Calf
(Continued from Page 38)

COW:

BODY: Use the #6 filbert brush to basecoat the body with Fawn. One coat is enough. Tint Raw Sienna with a little Titanium White, then paint over the basecoat; it will be slightly patchy.

Paint the darker patch on her rump with Burnt Umber. Paint Burnt Sienna on this patch, then paint tinted Burnt Umber on the patch here and there.

Use Raw Sienna + Burnt Umber (1:1) and the filbert brush to shape the pelvic bones. Pat the darker area on her lower stomach with full-strength Burnt Umber.

Tint Raw Sienna and glaze over her body to blend the other colours. Use the dirty brush to pick up Titanium White, then highlight along the top of back and bones. Use the liner brush to paint Burnt Sienna hair on the top of her back, above her head. Add more hair with Burnt Umber.

HEAD: Using the #3 round brush, basecoat the dark area of the face with Carbon Black + Burnt Umber (1:1), the jaw line with Raw Umber, the top of the head with Raw Sienna, the inner ears with tinted Raw Sienna, the outer area of the ear on the left with Burnt Umber, and around the nose with Nimbus Grey.

Dark Area of Face and Jaw Line: Use a tint of the basecoat mix and the #3 round brush to drybrush highlights on the dark area of the face. Use a tint of Raw Umber to highlight the jaw line. Drybrush Raw Sienna on a small section of the jaw line near the ear.

Top of Head: Use the liner brush to paint Burnt Sienna strokes for hair. Tint Raw Sienna to paint the lighter patch by the ear on the right. The small patch near the ear on the left is Warm White. Add hair on the very top of the head with Burnt Umber.

Ears: Use the liner brush to paint a small patch of Burnt Sienna inside the ear on the right. Paint around the edge of this ear and indicate the hair in the ear with Burnt Umber. Paint some lighter hair with tinted Raw Sienna.

Drybrush Burnt Sienna inside the left ear. Tint Raw Umber to paint the edges, then brush this colour on the outer section of the ear to highlight. Add additional Titanium White to the mix to intensify the highlight. Tint Raw Sienna and brush this on the lighter patch inside the ear.

Nose: Use the #3 round brush and Burnt Umber to basecoat the nose. Tint Burnt Umber to highlight the nose. Highlight the lighter area around the nose with full-strength Titanium White. Use the liner brush and Carbon Black to paint the nostril. Paint highlights around the nostril and on the nose with Titanium White.

Eyes: Use the liner brush. Basecoat the shape of the right eye with Burnt Sienna. The pupil is Carbon Black with a Titanium White highlight. Paint the lighter area of fur around the eye with tinted Raw Umber; highlight with a lighter tint of Raw Umber. Define the eyelid and under the eye with Carbon Black. Paint fine eyelashes with Titanium White. The left eye is Carbon Black with Burnt Sienna eyelashes.

AREA UNDER THE NECK: Use the #3 round brush and Burnt Umber to paint the layers for the neck to the right of the face and the section just under the nose. Paint the chest area with Fawn, then paint patches using the liner brush and Burnt Umber. Paint a few patches with Raw Sienna, then brush Titanium White on the left side. Paint a fine highlight line up the side of the neck to the right of the head with tinted Burnt Umber. Use this also to paint the highlight just under the nose.

LEGS: Basecoat the left side of the legs with Fawn using the #3 round brush. Basecoat the dark side of the legs with Burnt Umber; highlight with tinted Burnt Umber on the left side of the dark areas and just above the hooves. Use the liner brush to highlight the lighter side of the legs with tinted Fawn. Basecoat the hooves with Burnt Umber and highlight with tinted Burnt Umber.

CALF: Basecoat the calf, including head, with Burnt Sienna. Use the #3 round brush to paint the darker areas on the calf with Burnt Umber: on the two hind legs, on the right front leg, on breast area, around the neck, on the face and in the ears.

BODY AND LEGS: Use the #6 filbert brush. Work wet-on-wet, back and forth through the following colours using a dirty brush and full-strength paint. Don't completely cover the Burnt Sienna basecoat; allow some of this colour to show through.

Randomly paint over the calf with Raw Sienna. Pat tinted Raw Sienna on highlight areas. Add more Titanium White to the mix to intensify highlights. When you are happy with the body, use a liner brush to paint fine strands of hair around the edges of the front legs with Warm White.

HEAD: Use the #3 round brush, the liner brush and full-strength paint to add the details on the head. Tint Raw Sienna and use this to add highlights to the face and ears. Use the liner brush to paint Burnt Sienna hair down the centre of the face. The area around the nose is basecoated with Nimbus Grey, then highlighted with Warm White. Paint fine hair on top of the head and in the ears with Burnt Umber and then with Warm White. Use the Warm White to define the ears.

Basecoat the nose with Burnt Umber using the #3 round brush. Use the liner brush to paint Carbon Black in the nostril on the left and on the right side of the nose. Tint Burnt Umber and use the #3 round brush to drybrush highlights on the nose. Use the liner brush to add final highlights with Warm White.

The eyes are painted with the liner brush. Basecoat the shape of each eye with Burnt Sienna. The pupil is Carbon Black. Add a highlight to the pupil and paint the section in the front of each eye with Warm White. Paint eyelids with tinted Raw Sienna. Outline the eyes and eyelids with Burnt Umber.

GROUND AND GRASSES: Use the dry fan brush and full-strength Burnt Umber to paint the area underneath the grass and flowers. Just tap the brush on the surface to create the shape of the fan over and over, overlapping the brush strokes. This will create texture. Tint Burnt Sienna and lightly paint over this area, allowing the colour underneath to show through.

Paint the grasses with the #3 round brush and the liner brush. Apply strokes of Raw Umber, Olive Green and Naples Yellow Hue.

FLOWERS IN GRASS: Use the #3 round brush to paint the flowers freehand. Load the brush with Pacific Blue + Dioxazine Purple (1:1), then tip into Warm White and paint flowers by dabbing up and down in a relaxed manner.

BANNER: Transfer the pattern. Basecoat the front of the banner with tinted Raw Sienna; apply enough coats for opaque coverage. Basecoat the back of the banner and the cracks along the top with Burnt Umber.

Use the #4 flat brush to apply a thin coat of retarder on the front of the banner. Using the same brush, shade with Burnt Umber. Dry with the hair dryer and repeat as necessary.

Paint the highlights on the front of the banner in the same manner with Warm White. Highlight the back of the banner with Red Earth. Use the liner brush to define the edges with Warm White. Use the angled shader brush to float Burnt Umber narrowly around the edges of the banner.

WHEAT AND BLUE FLOWERS: Refer to the colour worksheet. Use the #3 round brush to basecoat the wheat with Raw Sienna. Use the liner brush to highlight the inner edge of each individual segment with tinted Raw Sienna. Outline and paint the wispy strokes and stems with thinned Burnt Umber.

Paint the blue flowers by loading the #3 round brush with the colour used for the flowers in the grass and dipping the tip of the bristles into Warm White. Press the brush to the surface to form the flowers. Use tinted Olive Green and the liner brush to add the stems and tendrils.

LETTERING: Transfer the lettering. Use the Rekab round brush to paint the lettering with thinned Burnt Umber, using as many coats as necessary for opaque coverage.

FINISHING DETAILS: Flyspeck the bucket with thinned Burnt Umber.

FINISHING

Refer to "Finishing" in the General Instructions at the front of the book.

Country Living Cow
Tray
Colour Photo on Back Cover

PALETTE
JO SONJA'S ARTISTS' COLOURS
Burnt Sienna
Burnt Umber
Carbon Black
Dioxazine Purple
Gold Oxide
Hookers Green
Nimbus Grey
Pacific Blue
Paynes Grey
Raw Sienna
Raw Umber
Red Earth
Smoked Pearl
Ultramarine Blue
Warm White
Yellow Deep
Yellow Oxide
JO SONJA'S BACKGROUND COLOURS
Galaxy Blue
Primrose
MATISSE ARTISTS' COLOURS
Skintone Light

BRUSHES
Angled Shader: 1/2"
Deerfoot: #4
Filbert: #6
Flat: #4, 1"
Liner: #10/0
Rake: 1/4"
Rekab Series 337 Round: #4
Round: #3, #10

SUPPLIES
Foam brush, 2"
Jo Sonja's Gesso, Black
Jo Sonja's Retarder Medium

This painting is based on an original photograph by Peter Asprey. Web site: www.cowphotos.com.

PREPARATION
Refer to Wood Preparation at the front of the book to prepare the craftwood using Method #2. After the gesso has dried, basecoat with Galaxy Blue. When dry, transfer the pattern for the cow, omitting the banners, wheat and flowers at this stage.

(Continued on Page 44)

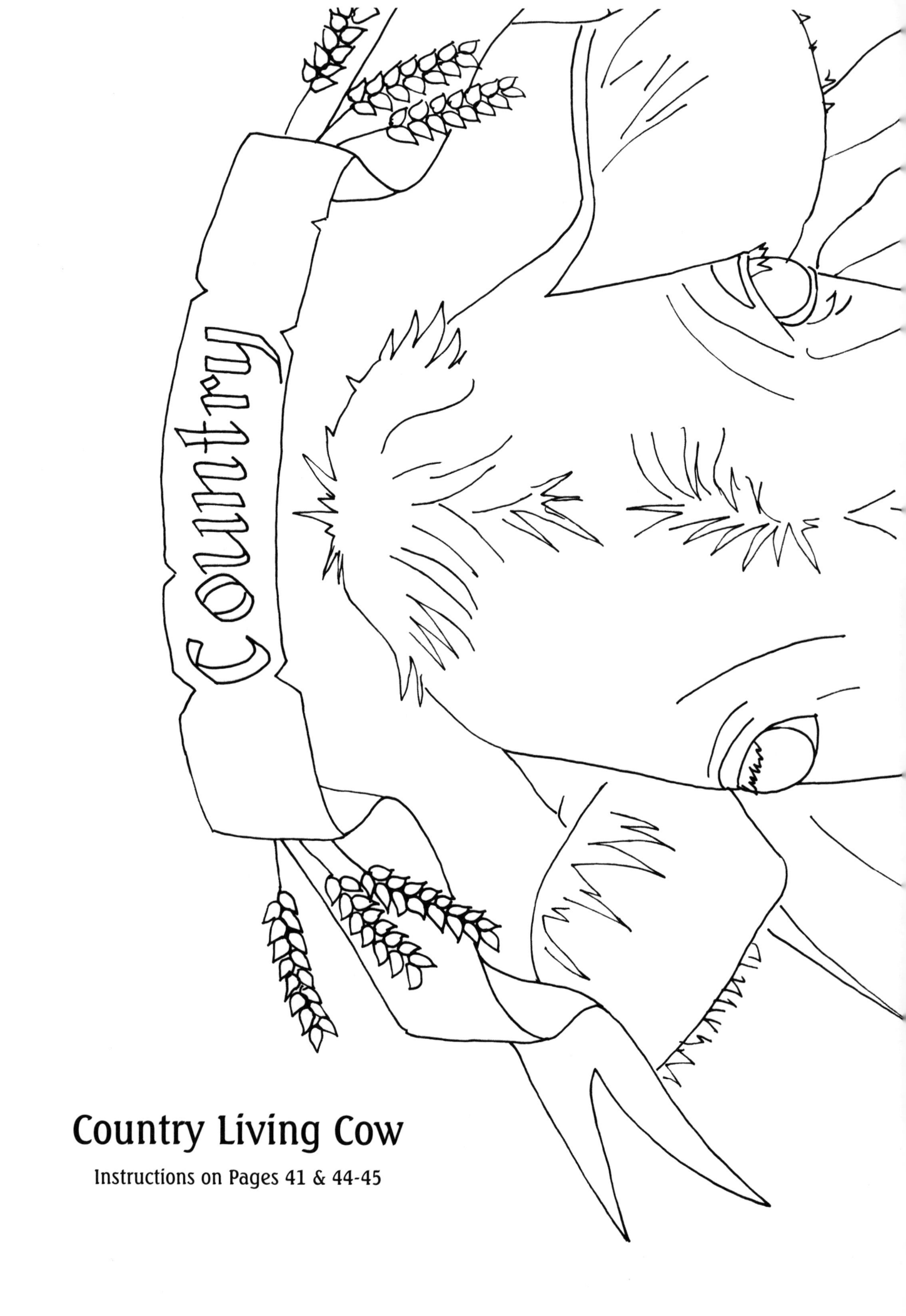

Country Living Cow

Instructions on Pages 41 & 44-45

43

Match and attach with
the pattern section on
pages 44-45

Country Living Cow

Match and attach with the pattern section on pages 42-43

Country Living Cow
(Continued from Page 41)

PROCEDURE

COW: Basecoat the face and the white markings on the right side of the cow with Nimbus Grey. Basecoat the ears and the body with Burnt Sienna. Basecoat the small section on the left side of the cow, just under the ear, with Warm White.

Using Burnt Umber + Ultramarine Blue (1:1), paint the darker areas in the ears, and below and to the right of the head.

Use the #6 filbert brush to begin adding layers of highlights and texture on the ears and body by applying Raw Sienna over the Burnt Sienna basecoat. Tint Burnt Sienna and continue to highlight the brown areas. Use Warm White to highlight the grey areas on the right side of the cow. Repeat the steps as necessary.

Use the #10 round brush to paint hair inside the ears with Burnt Sienna, then with Raw Sienna. Use the #3 round brush to paint finer hair inside the ears with tinted Raw Sienna and then Warm White. Use the rake brush to paint the hair around the edges of the ears with Raw Sienna, tinted Raw Sienna and then Warm White.

FACE: Use the #10 round brush to paint most of the texture on the face. Tint Paynes Grey and paint the darker areas on the cow's face. Add more Warm White to the mix and begin adding the hair down the middle of the face. Continue with the liner brush and Paynes Grey, followed by the #3 round brush and Smoked Pearl.

Use the #10 round brush to paint Smoked Pearl on both sides of the face. Paint over the Smoked Pearl on the left side of the face with Warm White. Paint Warm White on the upper, right side of the face with the #3 round brush. Use the #10 round brush to glaze Burnt Umber over the darker areas on the left side of the face, and on the right side of the face under the eye.

HAIR ON HEAD: The hair on the top of the head is painted with the #3 round brush and Burnt Umber + Ultramarine Blue (1:1). Follow this with Smoked Pearl and then Warm White.

Use the liner brush and Warm White to paint fine hair around the edges of the face and on the chin.

EYES: Basecoat the irises with Burnt Umber using the #3 round brush. Use the liner brush to paint the small section at the front of each eye with Warm White. Paint pupils with Carbon Black. The left eye has thinned Raw Umber painted above the eye on the eyelid. Outline around the left eye with Paynes Grey. The right eye has thinned Paynes Grey painted above the eye on the eyelid and underneath the eye. Paint a thin line of Burnt Umber along the top of each eye with the liner brush. The eyelashes are painted using the liner brush and thinned Nimbus Grey, followed by thinned Warm White. Paint the highlights in the eyes using the liner brush and thinned Nimbus Grey. When this is dry, paint Warm White highlights on top.

NOSE AND MOUTH: Basecoat the nose with Skintone Light. When dry, apply a thin layer of retarder over the nose. Use the #3 round brush to paint the nostrils by patting with Ultramarine Blue + Burnt Umber (1:1). Using retarder on the surface gives the paint a mottled, transparent effect. Use Paynes Grey + Skintone Light (1:1) and the filbert brush to paint the nose again, avoiding the area around the left nostril and a narrow area around the right nostril. Dry the nose with a hair dryer, then apply retarder again. Use the #3 round brush to pat the brown markings on the nose with Burnt Umber. Paint highlights on the left side of the nose around the nostril with Warm White.

Basecoat the mouth with Raw Umber. Use tinted Raw Umber to highlight. Use the angled shader to float Paynes Grey next to the right side and under the nose to form a shadow.

BANNER: Transfer the patterns for the banners. Basecoat the front of each banner with tinted Raw Sienna; apply enough coats for opaque coverage. Basecoat the back of each banner with Burnt Umber. Use the #4 flat brush to apply a thin coat of retarder on the front of the banner. Paint the shadows with Burnt Umber. Dry with the hair dryer and repeat the shading steps. Paint the highlights in the same manner with Warm White.

Highlight the back of the banner with Red Earth. Use the liner brush to define the edges of the banner with Warm White.

SUNFLOWERS: Transfer the sunflowers. Use the #3 round brush to basecoat the petals with Gold Oxide. Apply Yellow Oxide over the petals, pulling from the tip of each petal toward the centre, allowing the basecoat to show around the centre of the flower. Tint Yellow Deep and repeat this step. When dry, paint a glaze of Yellow Deep over the petals.

Use the deerfoot brush to stipple the centre of each flower with Burnt Umber. Pick up Red Earth with the dirty brush and stipple a highlight. Use the angled shader to float a Burnt Umber shadow on the petals around the centre of each flower. The tiny leaves at the back of each flower are basecoated with Hookers Green using the liner brush. Highlight with tinted Hookers Green. The tendrils are the same colour.

LETTERING: Transfer the lettering to the banner. Use the Rekab round brush to paint the letters with Burnt Umber. When dry, apply a second coat.

WHEAT: Refer to the coloured worksheet. Transfer the pattern for the wheat. Basecoat with Yellow Oxide using the #3 round brush. Using tinted Yellow Oxide and the liner brush, highlight the inner edge of each segment and paint the stems. Outline the segments using the liner brush and Burnt Umber. Paint the fine wispy strokes with the liner brush and Warm White.

PURPLE FLOWERS: The purple flowers are painted freehand. Mix Pacific Blue + Dioxazine Purple (1:1) and then tint this colour with Warm White. Load the #3 round brush with the mix and then dip the tip of the brush into Warm White. Press the brush to the surface to form the flowers. Use tinted Hookers Green and the liner brush to add the stems and small leaves.

FINISHING DETAILS: Use the #4 flat brush to paint the edge of the tray with Primrose. When dry, use sandpaper to lightly sand to allow the blue paint underneath to show through in places.

FINISHING

Refer to "Finishing" in the General Instructions at the front of the book.

Seed Box
Colour Photo on Page 49

PALETTE
JO SONJA'S ARTISTS' COLOURS
Burnt Umber
Cadmium Yellow Mid
Carbon Black
Dioxazine Purple
French Blue
Gold Oxide
Hookers Green
Moss Green
Naples Yellow Hue
Pacific Blue
Paynes Grey
Purple Madder
Raw Umber
Smoked Pearl
Teal Green
Titanium White
Yellow Oxide

BRUSHES
Angled Shader: 1/2"
Filbert: #6
Flat: #4, 1"
Liner: #10/0
Round: #3
Smudge Tint: #4

PREPARATION
My father made this little box for me from recycled western red cedar. There is no preparation needed. Transfer the pattern, omitting the peas, using very light pressure so you don't dent the surface of the wood.

PROCEDURE
Use Titanium White for tinting colours.

GRASSES: Paint the grasses freehand with the #3 round brush. Thin the colours slightly and use them in the following order: Burnt Umber, Paynes Grey, Moss Green, tinted Teal Green and Yellow Oxide. Using tinted Hookers Green and the liner brush, paint grass in front of the design after all other elements have been painted.

TERRA COTTA POTS: Refer to the colour worksheet. Basecoat with Gold Oxide using the #4 flat brush. When shading and highlighting, apply colour to the edge of the pot, then pull toward the middle, following the shape of the pot. Work through the following steps once, allowing each colour to dry, then repeat, working wet-on-wet without washing the brush between colours. If the paint on the brush starts to dry, just dip the brush into the water, but don't wash it.

Using Purple Madder + Gold Oxide (1:1) and the #4 flat brush, shade the right side of each pot. Tint Gold Oxide and highlight the left side of the pot. Brush Gold Oxide down the centre of the pot to blend the two previous colours together. Repeat the steps as necessary. Allow to dry.

Drybrush a small amount of Yellow Oxide on the left side of each pot. Mix Pacific Blue + Dioxazine Purple (1: touch)

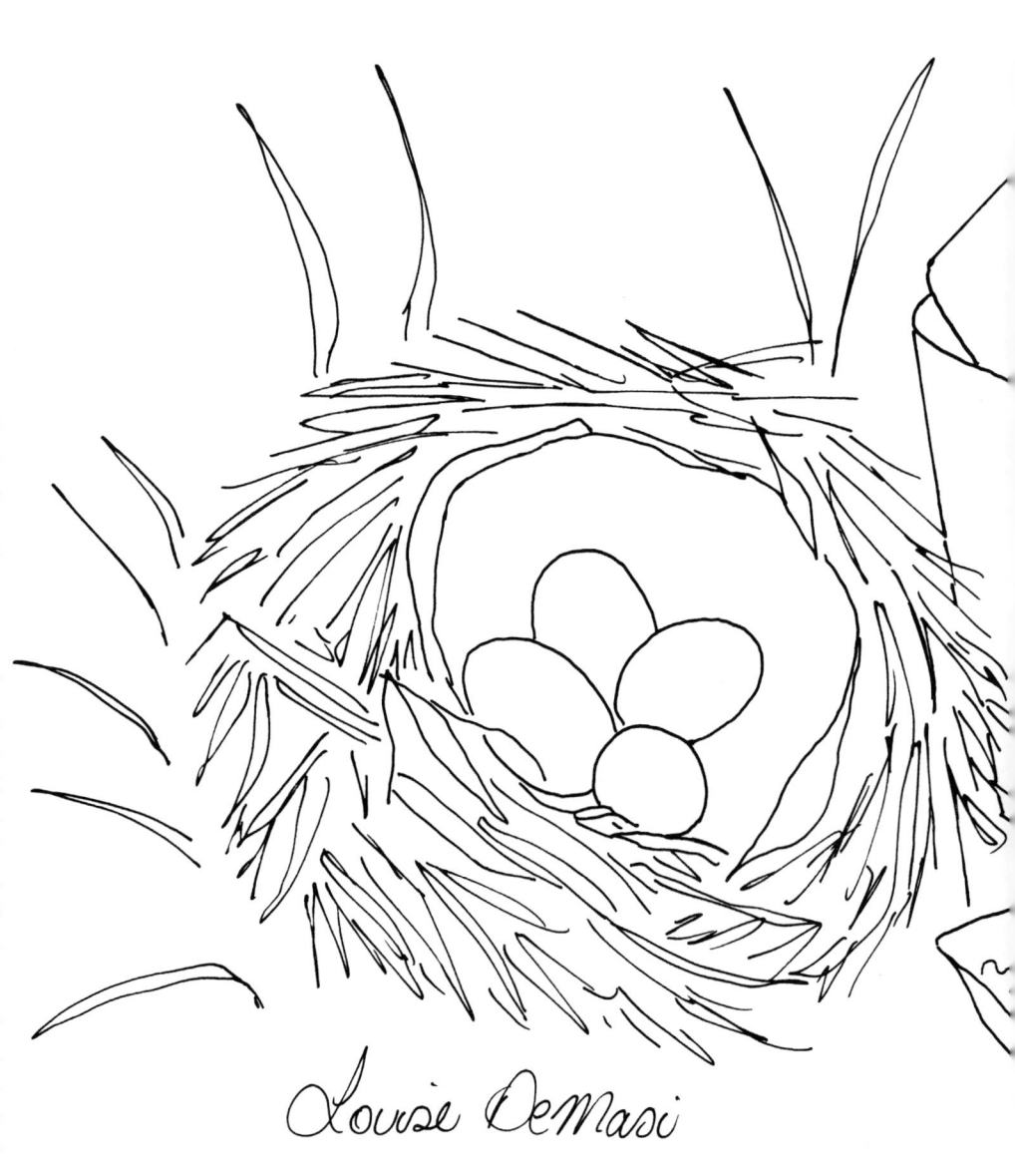

Louise DeMasi

and then tint the mix with Titanium White. Drybrush a tiny amount of this down the centre of each pot. Drybrush a small amount of Titanium White on the left side.

Float Paynes Grey shading inside each pot, along the rim. Shade the inside of the top pot with Purple Madder + Gold Oxide (1:1); drybrush tinted Gold Oxide highlights. Paint the crack with the liner brush and Burnt Umber. Use tinted Gold Oxide to outline and add definition to the rims of each pot.

NEST: Begin to form the outside shape of the nest by using the round brush to apply Burnt Umber strokes over the surface. Vary the thickness of the strokes. Next, paint a layer of Yellow Oxide strokes. Repeat with tinted Yellow Oxide.

Use the liner brush to paint some finer Burnt Umber strokes. You can define some of the heavier strokes by outlining them with Burnt Umber. Add a few Titanium White strokes with the liner brush, mainly in the front, left area.

The inside of the nest is painted with the same colours in the same order, but using the liner brush for much finer strokes. Paint Titanium White strokes on the lighter (right) side. Glaze a shadow on the left side with Carbon Black and the #3 round brush. When dry, repeat, covering a narrower area to intensify the shadow.

After painting the eggs, add some strokes over the eggs.

EGGS: Use the #3 round brush. Mix Teal Green + French Blue (1:1), then tint this mix with Titanium White to basecoat the eggs. Tint the mix further to drybrush highlights. Add more Titanium White to strengthen the highlight. Brush on a tiny amount of watery Titanium White as the final highlight.

Mix Pacific Blue + Dioxazine Purple (1: touch), then tint the mix with Titanium White. Drybrush a small amount on each egg. Use the angled shader to float Paynes Grey for the

(Continued on Page 48)

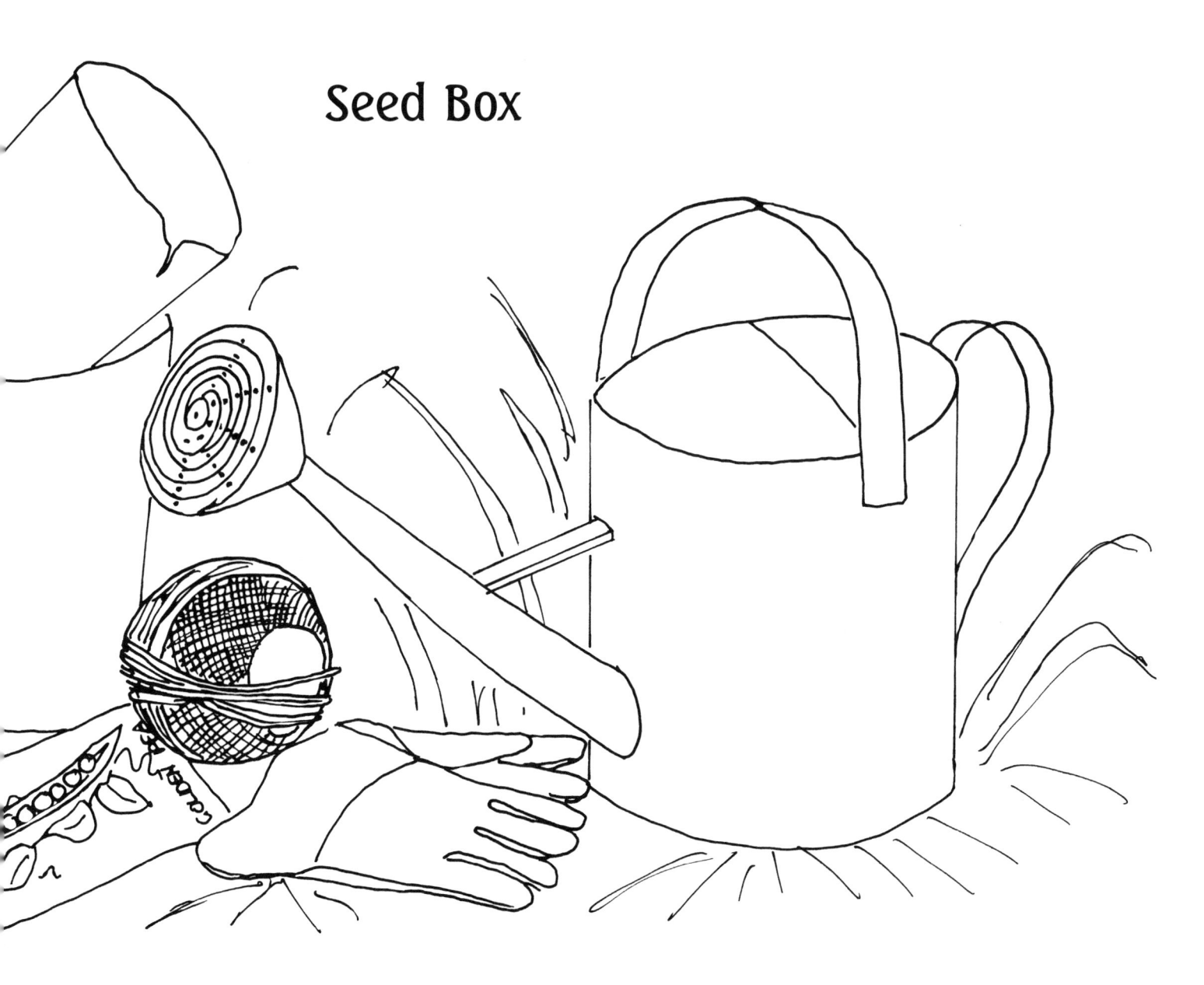

Seed Box

Seed Box

(Continued from Page 47)

shadows formed where one egg sits in front of another. Float Burnt Umber on the nest around the eggs.

SEED PACKET: Tint Yellow Oxide and basecoat the seed packet using the #4 flat brush. Add additional Titanium White to the mix, then highlight the front edge of the packet.

Transfer the pattern for the peas. Basecoat the pea pod and leaves with Hookers Green, using the #3 round brush. Use this brush to paint the peas with Moss Green. Using Cadmium Yellow Mid + Moss Green (1:1), highlight the top of each pea and the edge of the pod. Add a highlight of Titanium White to each pea with the liner brush.

Using the #3 round brush and Moss Green, highlight the leaves by applying colour to the edges, then pulling toward the centre. Paint the tendrils and stems with the liner brush and thinned Raw Umber. If you lose your dark colour on the leaves, outline and paint veins with Hookers Green.

Paint the lettering with Paynes Grey and the liner brush. Using the #3 round brush, drybrush the Dioxazine Purple/Pacific Blue/Titanium White mix used on the eggs on the packet. Use the angled shader to float Paynes Grey under the front and right edge of the packet for a shadow. Use the liner brush to outline the edges of the packet with Titanium White.

BALL OF STRING: Basecoat with Burnt Umber using the #4 flat brush. Basecoat the hole with Paynes Grey. You may need to transfer the details back onto the ball at this stage. Use the liner brush and thinned Yellow Oxide to paint the weave pattern of the string. Tint Yellow Oxide and highlight the string in the centre of the ball. Float Burnt Umber with the angled shader to form the shadows on and under the ball.

WATERING CAN: Basecoat the watering can with Paynes Grey + Titanium White (1:1); add more Paynes Grey to the mix to basecoat the inside of the can. Use the smudge tint brush to scumble the highlights. Make sure the brush is dry, and don't use a lot of paint. Lighten the basecoat mix with Titanium White to highlight the lighter areas on the left side and top of the watering can. Intensify highlights by picking up Titanium White with the dirty brush and repeating the step.

Use the #3 round brush to highlight the spout and handles with a tint of the basecoat colour. Indicate the indentations on the rose spray at the end of the spout using the #3 round brush and the highlight mix. Use the liner brush to paint the holes with Paynes Grey.

Use the smudge tint brush to scumble tinted Teal Green and tinted Gold Oxide here and there over the watering can. Do the same with Raw Umber. Use the angled shader to float Paynes Grey shading along the top and bottom edges of the watering can, and along the bottom edge of the spout. Use the liner brush and Titanium White to outline and define the light edges of the watering can.

GLOVES: Paint the orange section of the glove that's underneath the other with Gold Oxide + Purple Madder (1:1). The orange section on the front glove is basecoated with Gold Oxide. Use the #6 filbert brush and Purple Madder to shade and Naples Yellow Hue to highlight this section of the front glove.

The grey sections of the gloves are basecoated with Titanium White + Paynes Grey (2:1). Use the liner brush and Paynes Grey to paint the seams and shade the fingers. Use the #4 flat brush to highlight with Smoked Pearl. Strengthen the highlight with Titanium White. Use the smudge tint brush to scumble Raw Umber here and there.

FINISHING DETAILS: Float a Paynes Grey shadow with the angled shader on the grass behind the nest. Add a few Yellow Oxide strokes on the inside of the nest with the liner brush, pulling them over the shadow. Paint grass in front of the pots and watering can.

FINISHING

Refer to "Finishing" in the General Instructions at the front of the book.

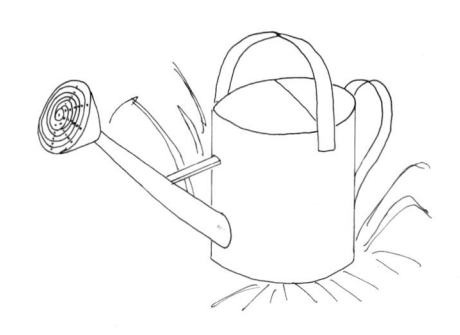

49

My Garden
Book
Pages 50-51

Seed Box
Pages 46-48

My Garden Book

Colour Photo on Page 49

PALETTE
JO SONJA'S ARTISTS' COLOURS
Burnt Umber
Cadmium Scarlet
Carbon Black
Dioxazine Purple
Gold Oxide
Hookers Green
Olive Green
Pacific Blue
Paynes Grey
Purple Madder
Raw Umber
Turners Yellow
Warm White
Yellow Oxide

BRUSHES
Angled Shader: 1/2"
Flat: #2, 1"
Liner: #10/0
Rekab Series 337 Round: #4
Round: #3

PREPARATION
Remove the front cover of the book by unscrewing the hinges. There is no preparation for this piece; I painted directly on the stained surface of the book. If your book is unfinished, refer to Wood Preparation in the front of the book, then stain with your favourite stain. Allow to dry, then flyspeck with Carbon Black. When dry, transfer the pattern, omitting the corn kernels for now.

PROCEDURE
CORN: Use Purple Madder to basecoat the area where the kernels will be painted. Allow to dry, then transfer the kernels. Use either the #3 round brush or the liner brush to basecoat each corn kernel with Turners Yellow, leaving the purple between kernels for shadows. You will need at least two coats. Use thinned Raw Umber to shade some of the kernels, then highlight the left side of some with Warm White.

Basecoat the corn leaves with Olive Green. Use the #3 round to drybrush various tints of Olive Green to form highlights; the Olive Green basecoat will form the shadows. Use the liner brush to paint a few streaks of Turners Yellow here and there, then paint the wispy strokes on the tips of the leaves with thinned Warm White.

STEMS: The stems at the base of the arrangement are basecoated with Hookers Green. Using tinted Hookers Green and the liner brush, start defining each stem; allow the basecoat to form the shadows. Add more Warm White to the mix to increase the intensity of the highlights.

Basecoat the string wrapped around the stems with Yellow Oxide. Highlight with a tint of Yellow Oxide.

PURPLE FLOWERS: Basecoat with Dioxazine Purple + Pacific Blue (1:1). Let dry. Transfer any petal lines that may have been lost during the basecoating.

Use the #2 flat brush to add highlights and shadows to the petals. Use full-strength paint and don't wash your brush between colours. Work wet-on-wet, blending the colours together. Paint the darkest areas in the centre of each flower with Paynes Grey. Tint the basecoat mix and begin highlighting the petals, starting from the edges and pulling the lighter colour toward the middle. Add more Warm White to the mix to intensify the highlights.

Use the liner brush and a very light tint of the basecoat colour to define edges of petals. Add the centre of the flower with large Yellow Oxide dots and small Gold Oxide dots. Softly drybrush a touch of Yellow Oxide on some of the petals here and there. Use the angled shader to float Purple Madder here and there on the petals.

LILIES: Basecoat the lilies with Yellow Oxide using the #2 flat brush. Work wet-on-wet to highlight and shade the lilies. Use Cadmium Scarlet to shade the darkest areas on each lily, blending this into the Yellow Oxide. Tint Yellow Oxide to highlight, again blending this into the Yellow Oxide.

Define top and lightest edges with the liner brush and a very light tint of Yellow Oxide. Use the angled shader to float Purple Madder in the throat of each flower. Use the liner brush and Yellow Oxide to paint the little stamen showing in the throat of the middle lily; highlight with Warm White. If necessary, define the edge of the stamen with Burnt Umber.

SMALL FILLER BUDS: Basecoat the buds with Purple Madder. Use the liner brush and tinted Purple Madder for highlights, pulling the colour across the bud to form a spiral pattern; allow the basecoat to show for shadows. Highlight further with Warm White. Basecoat the stems and leaves using the liner brush and Hookers Green. Highlight with a tint of Hookers Green.

LETTERING: Basecoat the lettering with thinned, tinted Yellow Oxide, using the Rekab round brush. You will need two coats. Use the liner brush and Burnt Umber to paint a drop shadow to the left and below each stroke.

FINISHING
Refer to "Finishing" in the General Instructions at the front of the book. Assemble the book.

Country Living Cow
Pages 41-45

Cow and Calf
Pages 38-41

ISBN 1-58891-082-2

7 16866 79062 6

Made in the USA

My Garden Book

My Garden

Louise DeMaxi